It's All His

God's Financial Plan

It's All His

God's Financial Plan

Mark Howell

Copyright © 2013 by Mark Howell
All rights reserved
Printed in the United States of America

No part of this book may be reproduced or transmitted in any form or by any means electronic or mechanical including photocopying and recording or by any information storage or retrieval system except as may be expressly permitted in writing by the publisher or author.

ISBN 978-0-9895226-0-1

References
The Holman Illustrated Study Bible
Copyright 2006 by Holman Bible Publishers
Nashville, Tennessee. All Rights Reserved

Holman Christian Standard Bible
Copyright 1999, 2000, 2002, 2003
By Holman Bible Publishers

Typesetting by E.T. Lowe Publishing Co.
Interior and cover design by Keata Brewer

Contents

Acknowledgments	vii
Introduction	1
1. Simple Times	5
2. Yoke Up with a Good One	13
3. Everyone Has a Choice	22
4. God's Money	33
5. Different Paths to Success	43
6. Hard Work	49
7. Need a Hired Hand	59
8. You Wanna be a Rock Star	69
9. The Party Doesn't Last	81
10. A Career Restart	88
11. You're (I'm) Not Preaching to the Choir	99
12. No Debt	106
13. Hope is in the Lord	112
14. Give to the Lord What is His to Begin With	121
15. Gospel vs. Religion: Fear Not	130
16. Conclusion	139

Acknowledgments

From an early age I had an interest and love for music. I listened to the hit songs that were being played on our local AM station in the 1970s and sang along with an annoying voice that I am sure drove anyone around crazy. Visiting my grandmom's house frequently I would explore and listen to all my uncle's collection of albums. A fun and interesting hobby was to read and take in all the information that was in or on the album covers. Most of the albums in the collection were rock oriented so this was where my interest lay in my music choices.

Reading the album covers over the years, listening to the music and going to the concerts gave me aspirations of fame and notoriety that accompanies the rock star. Since I have a silent movie voice, a radio face and could barely play an audio cassette the reality was just that of a distant dream. Since I will never produce a recording and with the advent of digital technology from which most consumers receive their music, I will never have my album to tell a story or deliver the "thanks" to all the people along the way for their support. So this is will be my album cover.

I would like to thank all the people that have been a part of my life over the past 40 plus years. First of all my mom who would do anything and has done everything to get me where I am today. An unselfishness that can not be described. The people that have known me and her our whole lives are aware of what she has done for her only child. Thanks to my dad who helped develop me during my younger years and make me into a respectful and disciplined child growing up. His support and providing for me as a child is something I am very thankful. I want to thank my grandmom whom a spent a lot of time with and my mom's five younger brothers (uncles) that gave me guidance when I was young. I would like to thank my cousin Todd Humphreys, who was more like a brother growing up, for developing my love for sports and especially football as we played on our first team together. And all my other cousins that I shared many Thanksgiving and Christmas gatherings.

There have been many great friends over the years that provided many of good times. One event that included a lot of my long time friends being a part of was "Couch Tour '96." This was a short tour that lasted a few months after I had returned from a nine month working stint in California. I returned back east and during a short, brief period was in "resident transition." These people let me crash or campout for a day or two during this period. I would like thank my old friends Bill Caudill, Alan Bryant, Derrick and Kim Potter, Ken Wilson, along with Mike Muray, JD Inman, Ken Alphin, TR Schmitt, Kelly O'Malley, and Shannon Moran Hajec for all of their tour support. Also I would like to thank the rock 'n' roll team of B&G delivery, Blake Bachman and Greg Tobin, for using me as the third hand and gave me some much needed income. You all were great contributors to the tour and show and I would never have made it through those times without you.

Along with the tour supporters Bill, Alan, Derrick and Ken who were a big part of my younger years and entourage of the high school days, I would like to thank the rest of the old gang: Tim "Tree" Thompson, Pete Quick, Mark Garvin, Craig Noltkamper, Scott Henon, Phil Yates, and brothers Joe and Jeff Yates. Jeff, you left us way too early and hope you are up in Heaven watching over the old gang. And to all the friends I have met over the years that have been a big part of my life, all of you are the best a friend could have.

Lastly, I would like to acknowledge my immediate family that I share every happy, wonderful moment. My wife Shauna, who could not be more of a perfect match for me. She knows everything about me and probably knows most of my thoughts. It is a match I had always wanted and dreamed about. And as the saying my wife quotes often, "What was I doing with my worthless life before we had our children?" This could not be said any better. Our great, beautiful, talented, funny, and on and on describes how we feel about our Morrison Faith and Jake Thomas. We could not have ordered up two of the best kids that exist in two happy parent's eyes.

Most importantly I would like to thank God and Lord and savior Jesus Christ for all that you have given me and entrusted me with. To have You as a provider and protector in this walk of life has made for the best one could ever imagine.

Again, thanks to everyone that has been a part of my life all these years, I love you all.

Introduction

Whether it is food, pelts or currency, people have used some sort of bartering system to acquire goods since the beginning of time. The range of items that were traded was limitless. Today, most people use some sort or currency or monetary system to barter for their needs. Unless you have inherited a large chunk of cash or are the benefactor of some other steady flow of cash you are working toward the acquisition of money, or currency to provide for your household.

You will find as many views of personal wealth as there are bank accounts: Easy come easy go, You can't take it with you, A dollar down a dollar a week, Save it for a rainy day, It's burning a hole in your pocket. The best practical view, however, is to give a little, save a little and live on less than your current income.

This book is about taking a Best Practice approach and applying spiritual and biblical practices. Practices that will protect you from shortfalls and allow you to live comfortably without the typical concerns associated with money. No matter if you own your own company or work for someone else you have the ability to be where you want to be and live without the stress and worry of finances.

God created this world and everything in it is His. This is our main premise and everything in this book rides on that premise. It does not mean that last summer's vacation, your season football tickets, or the new vehicle you are driving is God's. You acquired your goods and services through a monetary transaction, but the root of all our means is from God. There is nothing wrong with taking a vacation, going to a ball game or driving a new vehicle but let's examine the path to experiencing these activities as God intended.

Living in the United States, you have the best opportunity to acquire wealth and live like no one else in the world. The United States is the largest free market country in the world and if you are willing to work hard you can set goals and obtain success more easily than anywhere else. Along with our capitalist economy we have a population with financial resources to maintain an open and prosperous marketplace for goods and services.

With such a large trade based market in the United States, one tool that is often used to promote or sustain a business is debt. Systems have been put in place to substitute revenue, income and cash on hand with loans, lines of credit and borrowed funds that lead to debt. Future projections and speculations are just that, a gambling way of thinking or hoping that something is going to be worth more in the future than it is worth today. Real wealth is calculated based on the value or worth of what is in your hand today.

> **Proverbs 22:7** The rich rule over the poor, and the borrower is a slave to the lender.

Many businesses and entities exist based on debt that can be levied on real property and assets. Borrowing money means that you no longer work for yourself. Your actions are now driven by the interest owed on the loan. If you are unable to pay the loan you lose the property and assets you used as collateral. The number one rule for financial security and sustaining what you have earned is to not borrow what you do not have. Instead, you should work hard to reach your goals by saving and not spending beyond your income.

Lenders call collecting interest "Easy Money." Remember, when you borrow money someone else is getting rich off the work of your hands. There are some exceptions, such as the purchase of a home. Few people can pay in full up front to purchase a house. Be conservative and buy something that can be paid off in the near future. Find a place that fits comfortably within your budget and gives you a cushion to pay more each month and accelerate the process of paying it off quickly. Seeking the limits and maxing out what you can qualify for is never a good plan. Live within your means and keep debt on the low end of the limits when buying your home.

We will delve into the pitfalls and perils of debt and credit later. This book covers the spiritual approach to God's way of dealing with finance, possessions and stewardship of what is all His to begin with. There is more to the equation when it comes to how much money we have, how financially stable we may be or how we serve ourselves in our lives.

> **Proverbs 22:4** The result of humility is fear of the Lord, along with wealth, honor, and life.

1

Simple Times

> **Proverbs 22:6** Teach a youth about the way he should go; even when he is old he will not depart from it.

The baby boomer generation was the first to see financial differences that began when they came of age and started to apply a mindset different from their parents'. Parents of baby boomers had lived in meager times and experienced financial heartaches that have not been seen since the depression era. People living prior to the 1940s saw things that all generations to follow could not comprehend. Shortages of food and money are things we take for granted in the United States and only people that lived through a depression can relate to this experience.

After World War II the financial turn around was more than evident with a surging economy resulting from our victory in the war. We saw a boom not only in our economic prospects but in our population from the baby boom after the war. The baby boom era officially started after the war, in 1945, and ended in 1964. I was born in 1965 and knew a lot of kids that were in the grade ahead of me. They were a year older, born in 1964, and they all seemed to trend as being the youngest child in their household. There were a few exceptions but for the most part they were the last in line as baby boomers in their family.

Generation X describes the next generation group that was born from 1965 through 1979. Being born in the second month of 1965 makes me one of the oldest Generation X-ers you can find. We were the first group to really experience all the modern conveniences that had arrived on the scene. Growing up, most households had one color television that received three network television channels and one telephone in the house but still had a lot more luxuries than all the other generations combined. As far as telephones go, my family was an exception to this limitation. My dad was an employee of the telephone company so we had a phone in every room in the house. Bell Telephone used to control every aspect of the phone business including the actual phones. If you wanted an additional phone it had to come from a phone man off of his truck. You could not go out and buy one at a department store and just plug it in like today. Deregulation and the breakup of the Bell system put an end to Ma Bell's monopoly on the phone system of the day.

With all the new luxuries the mindset of hard work seemed to be less important than in previous years. The in demand luxuries and "I have to have it now," along with "I can pay for it later" with the credit plan became instilled in our lives. With the introduction of expanded credit opportunities we started to go beyond our limits.

As a child in the 1970s I experienced the last decade of the "simple times." This was the last decade that economic disparity was at a minimum. Everyone was, for the most part, on the same economic level. Of course, there were a few families that had a little more and a few that had less than the average household. There were financial assistance programs in place but the area and economic landscape I grew up in did not show much evidence of these programs. If someone became unemployed they were quick to tackle the situation and found employment sooner rather than later. There was less of "What free programs can I take advantage of now?" and more pulling up the bootstraps and getting back on track.

> **Proverbs 20:4** The slacker does not plow during planting season, at harvest time he looks, and there is nothing.

In elementary school I knew there was a free lunch program but never knew who participated in the program. My school housed first through eighth grade which is unheard of in today's school systems. That school environment had kids that might have started school early at age five and kids that might have been held back a year at age 15, with full beards, roaming the halls and riding the buses together. Not until the eighth grade did I start to become aware of financial situations and then start to see some gaps in economic status.

Our eighth grade teacher would start the day by calling roll and collecting the daily lunch money from the students. When your name was called you would announce the number of days you were paying for that week. Lunches were 50¢ in the late '70s, so if it was Monday and you were paying for the whole week you would respond five days and take $2.50 to the classmates assisting the teacher. For the rest of the week when your name was called you would say "Paid" as your response to roll call.

During roll call was the first time I realized that there were students in the free lunch program. The one kid in my class that was in the program had to respond to the roll calls with "free lunch." I always felt bad for the humiliation and embarrassment the one kid had to endure every morning for his response and could not figure out why the teacher could not have implemented a better system. This student, however, was a pretty tough kid and no one would have ever called him out for the roll call response.

Even with kids on free lunches and the more fortunate kids like myself there was still not a lot of diversity in our school in the 1970s. Everyone pretty much wore the same clothes, drove the same cars and lived in the same style house. Very little varied from household to household throughout the neighborhoods across the city.

I grew up with two working parents that always had good stable jobs. As mentioned earlier, my dad worked for Bell Telephone until he retired and my mom always had a supervisory job in office administration. We were never a family in need or want and just cruised along, as did all the families of the day. As an only child I did have a few privileges that not all kids were afforded.

For Christmas in 1974 I got my first motorcycle, which was considered something of a luxury as not a whole lot of kids had a dirt bike. Prior to this I had a three-wheeler that was more of a lawnmower without a blade. It was a cool starter toy with a motor but it was not a motorcycle. After I outgrew the Honda XR-75 I moved up to a two stroke 1976 Suzuki RM-100. This would turn out to be a big jump from the four stroke mini bike to a screaming power band, two stroke dirt bike. My early experiences with motorcycles has made me a fan today of bikes and I believe all kids, boy and girls, should learn and experience the fun of motorcycles.

Another category of luxury items that not all kids were afforded was sporting gear. Kids all around were playing ball and had the basics to play and compete in sports but I had to have the top of the line gear in all my sporting activities. Pee Wee football leagues issued cheap plastic helmets with plastic facemasks that I suspect would not meet requirements for today's equipment standards. My parents would go to the sporting goods store at my request, and get as close as possible to a pro or college style helmet with a full cage metal facemask that was just like the pros wore on Sundays. I also had my own shoulder pads that were comparable to what the high school kids were wearing at the time. I had the mindset that if you looked good and professional you would be good. Then if you were not that good a player you would at least have the look.

One spring, before the Little League Baseball season, we were at the sporting goods store along with one of my best friends who was also on my team. I had picked out shiny white leather Pumas with the suede stripe, the hottest new cleats. They cost over $40, which was a lot for the period. My softhearted mom must have seen the look on my friend's face while I tried on my new pair of cleats for the season. To his surprise she asked him if he wanted a pair. He hollered out his size and we both had the coolest, best pair of cleats on the 1976 American Little League champion Angels. Twenty years later my friend came to my uncle's funeral and could not resist bringing up his memory of my mom buying him the leather Puma cleats that Little League season. Outside of my motorcycles and high end sporting gear, I really had no more than any other kid.

During the 1970s my family purchased three different homes. All three were basic, modern styles of the time. All had three bedrooms, two baths and a two-car garage. Prior to the first purchase of these three in 1971 we had lived in an older house that my parents bought in the late '60s. It was a starter house that was built in the 1940s with the basics of two bedrooms and one bath typical of the era. Another feature typical for the cottage style house was the single car garage with the carriage door that opened up and was just an extension of the gravel driveway.

Then along came the era of the two-car garage and wall-to-wall carpet. A major flaw with these houses was the carpet that covered every room of the house. Even the kitchens and bathrooms were carpeted back then. Carpeting areas with water present on a daily basis caused problems which would be figured out in later years. Walls consisted of a lot of paneling and the ceilings all had the sponge applied plaster. This was the style of the day and the costs were all within the set budgets so everyone was paying about the same price for one of these new houses.

The point is that you bought what you could afford. Everyone was more or less on the same playing field as far as income so everything was kept in check for affordable housing. You would put down 10% to 20% and get a shorter term than what is being offered in the open market. A fifteen or 20-year note would be all that was needed to purchase a family home. In the '80s and '90s financial instruments and programs evolved as the pricing climbed to levels never seen before in the industry. Long terms, balloon notes, adjustable rates and other inventive programs all came along to help people get into places they really could not afford.

Working in the mortgage industry from the late '90s until the housing bust in the late '00s, I told people that we were creating a monster with all of Wall Street's creative financing. Investors were throwing together ridiculous programs trying to keep the housing boom moving. These loan programs were considered acceptable by the industry and we sold them. If we did not offer them the customers would go to the next lender and get the loan closed. One of the most outrageous programs I remember was a stated, non-owner occupied, 100% purchase with a 620 credit score. What this meant was a person with a moderate credit rating could state their income (with no verification) and buy an investment property with no money down.

Proverbs 22:26-27 [26]Don't be one of those who enter agreements, who put up security for loans. [27]If you have no money to pay, even your bed will be taken from under you.

When people have no risk or initial investment in the purchase of a house what incentive do they have to make sure they are going to take care of the place? Inexperienced investors plan to get someone in to rent the place and hopefully this will cover the payment and a little extra for the "investor." However, frequently the tenant skips out or the owners cannot get a tenant in the place. Maintenance costs occur, and taxes and insurance are due. The solution for the owners then becomes to just let the place go. No investment equals no accountability.

This was the result of the real estate boom up until 2006. People have nothing invested and the values have dropped so why would they continue to make payments. Before the 1980s I rarely, if ever, heard of a foreclosure. Of course they were out there but people I knew lived within their means and had a greater sense of responsibility to carry out their obligations. Also banks and lending institutions were more cautious and made less risky, responsible business decisions when dealing with their clients.

The responsibility falls on the borrower's shoulders but when financial institutions offer mortgage options that lead people to overwhelming financial obligations it can only end badly. Everyone involved will ultimately lose when the obligations are not met. The lender that owns the mortgage will be able to repossess or foreclose. The borrower will acquire the negative impact of taking out credit that they should never have qualified for. The interest and compensation generated from these transactions keeps the lending cycle alive and people heaped under huge amounts of debt.

> **Proverbs 21:5** The plans of the diligent certainly lead to profit, but anyone who is reckless only becomes poor.

We all experience times when we do not know which way go or where to turn—times when desperation and fear come upon you. Whatever the difficulties, remember the least of them are your finances. Money and finances should be on the bottom rung of concerns. Compared with things such as a sick child, a troubled family member or a natural disaster the shortage or lack of money is a manageable problem. Finances should be a priority, but put them in perspective against other things that would be more devastating.

Your financial status should not be ignored but your focus on what is important should be prioritized relating to God's standards. His guidelines are very simple: work hard, give a little, don't borrow money, tend to the widows and orphans, and do not chase fantasies. Many common sense approaches are included in the financial guidebook from the Lord. With such a simple list of approaches to money why waste time concerning yourself with financial issues? Follow the rules designated by God.

Proverbs 3:5-6 [5]Trust in the Lord with all your heart, and do not rely on your own understanding; [6]think about Him in all your ways, and He will guide you on the right paths.

2

Yoke Up with a Good One

Proverbs 19:14 A house and wealth are inherited from fathers, but a sensible wife is from the Lord.

Your spouse is your partner in almost everything you do, especially where finances are concerned. If you are not on the same page financially you will struggle throughout your life making ends meet. I have met many people over the years that have been very successful in the business world but the spouse is on the opposite end of the spectrum regarding finances. You have one spouse who is frugal and contemplates each purchase before the cash is laid out. The other half of the team has no regard for money or budgeting and will spend until it is gone, reloading as soon as the next paycheck arrives.

Note that I did not specify either the husband or wife as spender or miser because it goes both ways. I have seen husbands slave only to see the wife go out and spend $700 on purses and $500 on shoes. On the other hand, I have also seen the wife conserve, clip coupons, buy inexpensive clothes and stretch a food budget only to see the husband go out and purchase a boat, a motorcycle and play four rounds of golf a week.

I have also seen other situations where the spouse is

oblivious to the whole financial condition of the household. Either by choice or the spouse that handles the household finances just does not include the other in any of the decisions or activities that involve the family budget. One spouse can be just rolling along without any knowledge or idea of what is happening with their finances. Hopefully everything is going smoothly and there is not a need to worry about anything financially. But in a lot of situations the spouse that is not involved is totally in the dark and when something goes terribly wrong with the family's finances they are blindsided. All of a sudden everything goes from not a worry in the world to their whole existence is upside down.

It is always recommended that spouses monitor and have equal control in the family budget. If one is left out or has an attitude of indifference a big surprise can be just around the corner. If you prepare and work together on finances and budgets you will have knowledge and input to what occurs within your household.

> **Proverbs 31:10-31** [10]Who can find a capable wife? She is far more precious than jewels. [11]The heart of her husband trusts in her, and he will not lack anything good. [12]She rewards him with good, not evil, all the days of her life. [13]She selects wool and flax and works with willing hands. [14]She is like the merchant ships, bringing her food from far away. [15]She rises while it is still night and provides food for her household and portions for her servants. [16]She evaluates a field and buys it; she plants a vineyard with her earnings. [17]She draws on her strength and reveals that her arms are strong. [18]She sees that her profits are good, and her lamp never goes out at night. [19]She extends her hands to the spinning staff,

and her hands hold the spindle. [20]Her hands reach out to the poor, and she extends her hands to the needy. [21]She is not afraid for her household when it snows, for all in her household are doubly clothed. [22]She makes her own bed coverings; her clothing is fine linen and purple. [23]Her husband is known at the city gates, where he sits among the elders of the land. [24]She makes and sells lined garments; she delivers belts to the merchants. [25]Strength and honor are her clothing, and she can laugh at the time to come. [26]She opens her mouth with wisdom, and loving instruction is on her tongue. [27]She watches over the activities of her household and is never idle. [28]Her sons rise up and call her blessed. Her husband also praises her: [29]"Many women are capable, but you surpass them all." [30]Charm is deceptive and beauty is fleeting, but a woman who fears the Lord will be praised. [31]Give her the reward of her labor, and let her works praise her at the city gates.

A lot of these references refer to the life of a woman in ancient times. But in a lot of the situations described above you can plug in to the lives of women today. I can relate to my wife's actions in every verse written in Proverbs 31. When I think of her daily actions and involvement with people, work and family she carries out the instructions that God has handed down to describe the spiritual woman.

My wife may not be out sewing garments and preparing cloth for the market place but she is out working to benefit the family. In fact, she is probably the best businesswoman I have ever come across. When I first met her, she was in a sales support role for corporate sales. She and I attended a company function hosted by her local staff and sales team. After being around salesmen that were highly compensated in the firm it became clear that she was way more competent and qualified than these people. I asked her why was she working for these people instead of pursuing the sales role for herself.

Within a couple of months a competing company hired my wife and she proceeded to bury her former employer by out-working and out-selling her former colleagues. After going into sales she became not only a leader locally but nationally within her industry. Her work ethic is inspirational to me and I hope it will be passed on to our children. A strong work ethic is a trait that must be developed at a young age. Once old enough, a child should have responsibilities in the form of chores or a job to instill a work ethic and establish a sense of responsibility.

Children, at a young age, should learn and appreciate the value of a dollar. A rule my wife and I are instituting is that if you are not playing sports or involved in any other extracurricular activity you are going to have a job. Our children are still young but even at elementary levels the demand of managing time and schedules can be hectic. If they are still playing at the high school level I will give them the luxury of balancing just these activities along with their studies. Once there is no participation in extracurricular activities, however, is when the work life begins. Nothing comes from idle time, no responsibility and no one to answer to.

> **Proverbs 10:4** Idle hands make one poor, but diligent hands bring riches.

My wife and I are both only children and, in a strange coincidence, both of our dads worked for and retired from phone companies. Her mom stayed at home and ran a tight ship as far as managing the meals, household and immediate home related duties. My mom always worked from the day she was 15 and still works three days week. When I was growing up it was not that common to have both parents working. Both of my parents had good jobs so money was not necessarily tight but we were not rich by any means. Being an only child, however, I did see some of the extras that were not afforded to some.

My wife's parents lived very conservatively, saving and taking control of any expenses that came their way. The only debt they ever had was their house, which was paid off in a short time and was where they lived until my wife was grown. Later, when my wife was in college, her parents built another house that was more accommodating for her mom who had developed debilitating arthritis. After my wife and I married, her parents sold their house in east Tennessee and moved to be near us outside of Nashville. Because of their wise financial choices, they had enough money to pay cash for their new house and still have some cash left over.

Not long after the birth of our second child my wife's mom passed away. We were both happy that she was near us and able to hold and nurture both her grandkids. She had a big influence on them both in the short time she had to be with them. Soon after, my wife's dad put his house into a trust for our kids. Being a good Christian man, he made good on what it says in scripture about your children and grandchildren.

> **Proverbs 13:22** A good man leaves an inheritance to his grandchildren, but the sinner's wealth is stored up for the righteous.

I had a privileged childhood and always had what was needed or wanted. My parents had enough disposable income to provide for many luxuries. Their marriage did not last but they did stay together until I was a freshman in high school, which was a tremendous benefit to me. For younger children in grade school it is very important to have a two parent family structure. I remember kids with single parents that did not live in a neighborhood but in an apartment or trailer home. By the time I was in high school I was ready to become more independent and less concerned about the family unit than I was in grade school.

Fortunately, my parents had an amicable split and there were not even any requirements for alimony, child support, etc. They mutually agreed that my dad would continue to make the house payment and once sold I would receive any proceeds from the sale. When the last house my parents purchased together was sold in 1992 I got my inheritance and packed my bags for Nashville. I was young and did not manage the money well and quickly blew through the funds in a matter of months.

Luke 15:11-21 [11]A man had two sons. [12]The younger of them said to his father, "Father give me the share of the estate I have coming to me." So he distributed the assets to them. [13]Not many days later, the younger son gathered together all he had and traveled to a distant country, where he squandered his estate in foolish living. [14]After he had spent everything, a severe famine struck that country, and he had nothing. [15]Then he went to work for one of the citizens of that country, who sent him into his fields to feed pigs. [16]He longed to eat his fill from the carob pods the pigs were eating, but no one would give him any. [17]When he came to his senses, he said, "How many of my father's hired hands have more than enough food, and here I am dying of hunger! [18]I'll get up, go to

> my father, and say to him, Father, I have sinned against heaven and in your sight. ¹⁹I'm no longer worthy to be called your son. Make me like one of your hired hands." ²⁰So he got up and went to his father. But while the son was still a long way off, his father saw him and was filled with compassion. He ran, threw his arms around his neck, and kissed him. ²¹The son said to him, "Father, I have sinned against heaven and in your sight, I'm no longer worthy to be called your son."

By no means do I have any complaints about my childhood. However, the divorce did set my mom and dad back financially. By calculating their contributions and time spent with their respective companies, they would have retired with substantially more cash as well as a comfortable pension for monthly needs. The last house they purchased would have long been paid off and it probably would have been a little easier existence.

Again, I am not complaining about their divorce but showing what a divorce can do financially. There are times when a divorce is the only recourse but in almost every situation there will never be a winner financially. Even if someone is granted a large sum of money in a divorce rarely is it conserved and it does not become a blessing to the beneficiary. Cash quickly gained is usually quickly spent.

> **Proverbs 28:25** A greedy person provokes conflict, but whoever trusts in the Lord will prosper.

Having a spouse that is not on the same page financially can be as major an issue as having one not willing to join you spiritually in your walk with God. I have a long time friend who has worked hard for years and has built businesses into successful companies from the ground up. He had Christian beliefs instilled into him at a young age. He worked hard, prayed and put everything he had into his business. When he made some mistakes along the way he had the ability to bounce back and keep rolling. His wife, however, took full advantage of what money did come in and burned through it quickly. Now, my friend does not regularly attend or belong to a church and seems too distraught over his marital situation.

Recently, the same friend got a divorce and his company has been caught up in the aftermath of the failed marriage. It is obvious that he is the leader of the company and the company's success comes from his knowledge, acquired over the years of operating the business. If the company is split and each spouse has equal control of operations it will only be a matter time before his former wife will wreck the company. Being the good businessman that he is, I think my friend will be able to salvage what is left of the company through control allocations made in the divorce agreement. This is another example of how there are no winners when a divorce is a part of your life.

My wife and I went out with the couple described above a while back and something his wife said stuck with me. We were talking about church, tithing and other related topics, and she made the statement, "Oh, you pay fire insurance." It took me a minute, then I got it, you are only paying your tithe so you will not end up in hell. That pretty much gave the whole story of her views of the church and Christianity. I never really thought that much about it until recently when my friend was telling me about his current situation. You cannot reach the ultimate goal of being a part of God's everlasting glory if you are yoked up with a non-believer.

It not only applies to husbands and wives but to other segments of your life as well. I have a friend who is a doctor and was in a very successful practice. He felt the work environment was deteriorating because he and the other doctors were not on the same page concerning their objectives and practices. After much deliberation he decided to go out on his own. He was leaving behind a prosperous practice that had great promotion and marketing and was highly successful. In the end, however, he felt it was just not worth it to be associated with people who operated on a non-believer track and worked only for themselves and their families but not also for the glory of the Lord.

---

2 Corinthians 6:14-15 [14]Do not be mismatched with unbelievers. For what partnership is there between righteousness and lawlessness? Or what fellowship does light have with darkness? [15]What agreement does Christ have with Belial?

3

Everyone Has a Choice

> Proverbs 12:14 A man will be satisfied with good by the words of his mouth, and the work of a man's hands will reward him.

You can never go wrong with hard work. I have known people with minimal incomes but who have lived right financially, not getting overextended and living on what they had. Not using credit and paying as you go is another practice that will help you succeed in reaching your financial goals. The best practice to assure that you will have the ability to function financially is to honor the Lord with your first fruits and apply His practices to money and living in this world with money.

There will always be poor people among us. This is even stated with almost the exact same wording in two different verses. This statement is in stone. Jesus himself delivers this message not only to make the point that not everyone will have the advantage of being rich, but also to make it clear that people will not always have Him. Meaning, if you do not have Jesus with you, rich or poor, living in a mansion or living in a van down by the river, your life is nothing without the Lord. What good is it to gain the world and lose your soul in the process? The streets of heaven are paved with gold and gates of pearls so what good is your wealth and possessions in the eyes of God?

> **Matthew 26:11** You always have the poor with you, but you do not always have Me.

> **John 12:8** For you always have the poor with you, but you do not always have Me.

This scripture does not mean that if you are doing fine in your existence what does it matter that poor are around you. You will have many occasions to make a difference in the life of someone not as fortunate as you financially. Based on 2005 U.S. Census Bureau statistics only 1.5% of the United States households makes $250,000 or more per year. People so fortunate to make an income of over $250,000 have a chance to touch or help the lives of over 98.5% of the people around them. Your giving opportunities may take many forms and you need to decide what your actions will be in your quest to help God's people.

> **Proverbs 19:17** Kindness to the poor is a loan to the Lord and he will give a reward to the lender.

> **Proverbs 28:27** The one who gives to the poor will not be in need, but the one who turns his eyes away will receive many curses.

You do not have to be in the 1.5% range, making a great income, to help those in need. It is amazing what a little can do for people who have little or nothing. By passing forward the blessings you have been awarded or entrusted with by the Lord you will not only have the blessing of the joy of giving but also the reward God promises you for carrying out His word.

Just because you may have been brought into this world poor or your current situation might deem you financially poor does not mean you have to continue on that path. The roads are paved with opportunities that are rewarded with hard work. Over time the United States is full of stories of people that came from nothing and made themselves into famous individuals on many fronts of activities. There is no limit to what can be accomplished when someone strives and puts in the effort to hit their goals.

But the same can be said for not working hard or not working at all. If you are an able-bodied individual and have no limitations on working you should be out there attempting to make you own living. During recent years the United States has become more and more of an entitlement state. There is more government assistance than any other time in our history. And recently it has increased due to the number of people that have been added to the various programs available. The number of people on some form of government assistance is staggering.

I am not saying there should not be some form of financial assistance in our country. But I do know not everyone receiving benefits should be eligible to get them, especially if they are capable of working. You can scan almost every large communities' jobs postings and discover hundreds of jobs being offered at any giving time. Most of these are probably not dream jobs but they do offer employment and in a lot of cases a means to an end. Anything in the form of employment you acquire is going to be much better than the minimal amounts of government assistance one may be receiving.

> **Proverbs 20:13** Don't love sleep, or you will become poor; open your eyes, and you will have enough to eat.

For the most part, I have always had an entrepreneurial spirit, wanting to branch out, operate independently and have my own business. I have had some successes but have also chased some dreams (or in some cases fantasies) that never made it to fruition. They were great opportunities but I was distracted thinking I could accomplish too many things at once. If you spread yourself thin you will lose focus on your aspirations. To become something bigger you must keep sight of the basics that created your initial success. I have been distracted myself in the past, and lost focus of key areas within my business. This is detrimental if you do not have the plans in place to execute your next steps.

I have had some ideas that could have been successful if I had put all my attention and efforts into the prospective business. However, that meant putting lack luster effort towards my existing work. If you are out on your own you better be prepared to work and dedicate your efforts to the business at hand. Work is hard enough when someone else employs you. As a business owner you manage all the moving parts. All the final decision making comes from you as the owner.

If you lose focus on your goals you are not going to be successful in the long run. Yes, you might limp along and squeeze out a living but if you are planning for the long haul you need long term planning. However good your business plan is there is never going to be a substitute for hard work. Also, if you are going to pour everything you have into a business and work nonstop you better make sure you are working smart at the same time. You can work your fingers to the bone but if you are not working effectively you will just be spinning your wheels.

Being in business for yourself is not an easy task. There are the rewards of being independent and keeping all your earnings but never forget that the buck starts and stops with you. Make sure you have a plan with all the checks and balances in place to accommodate for the ups and downs in a business. Rest assured, you will experience every up and down that can come about as a business owner.

Most people have had an idea to go out on their own and try to start a business or venture with a new product or service. You may not have experienced the entrepreneurial spirit but you probably know someone who has. It may not always be the easy route to success that you perceive it to be. If you want to make that move the first thing needed to start is a business plan. If you do not have a plan of attack you are only setting yourself up for disaster and failure in the end. If an initial plan is not set in place, and if the plan is not followed, it will slow down the process. If the path is not righted it will become more and more difficult to gain the momentum needed to make the venture successful.

Now, lets talk about what happens if you have a good business plan and the tools needed to get your business off the ground. Every business in existence today had to start somewhere. You might have an idea where you are taking something from scratch and basically starting a brand new venture from the ground up. Or it just might be an existing concept or business you feel you can improve on and make a better product or service from your efforts. Whatever the case may be make sure you have covered every base of what is laid out in your plan. There are many moving parts to a business plan so it is up to you to make sure you prepare for every possible outcome.

Remember there are good times and bad times in every business, how you plan for each will ultimately dictate how well you succeed. Have back up plans for your back ups and hopefully you will be on the positive side of the business world. The U.S.

Census Bureau states that 51% of small businesses survive five years. So looking into the business crystal ball you have around a 50/50 chance of making five years with a new small business. After five years the trends become more in favor of the business owner and your chances of staying around increase each year until it levels off at a 70% success rate.

Luke 12:48 Much will be required of everyone who has been given much. And even more will be expected of the one who has been entrusted with more.

This short verse is one I have recently become more aware of and am trying to take more to heart. God has already given us much by giving us the life and air in our lungs. Living in the United States of America is another gift that most people in the world do not have the privilege to enjoy. We are given many opportunities to excel and carve out a path in whatever we want to pursue. Unfortunately, many do not take advantage of the opportunities that surround us in this country that offers so much.

Being a youth league coach I like to use Luke 12:48 to help younger players and, hopefully, future followers of Christ, receive this message. The younger the team you are coaching the wider the range of abilities you are going to have. Some of the players are just being introduced to the sport and their abilities are limited. For these players, instructional coaching is going to be the main focus of the season. There are others that will have the experience or just natural ability to play the game. I try to give everyone equal attention while coaching during the season but I will use different techniques or levels of training based on the abilities of the players. One of the first things I do is pull the advanced players to the side and let them know what is expected of them during the year. I lay out the scripture for them that where much is given more is going to be required. They have been given the talent and ability to play ball, and with that talent I am going to be demanding and expecting more out of them on the field. I will push a little harder and sometimes be a little more vocal than I would with the less experienced players. By doing this I hope I can get them to excel and take full advantage of gifts and talents that are God given.

Doing the most with your God given gifts not only applies to playing ball but also the many other talents that we may possess. It might be academic, artistic, physical or any other category of talent, but whatever the case we need to make sure we give all we have to maximize our full potential. Years down the road you do not want to hear the phrase "waste of talent" directed toward you.

> **Titus 1:7-9** [7]For an overseer, as God's manager, must be blameless, not arrogant, not quick tempered, not addicted to wine, not a bully, not greedy for money, [8]but hospitable, loving what is good, sensible, righteous, holy, self-controlled, [9]holding to the faithful message as taught, so that he will be able both to encourage with sound teaching and to refuse those who contradict it.

Being a business owner I had the opportunity to be the manager of an organization. The attitudes a manager displays in a position of authority shows his true personality and inner makeup. God is looking for how you handle these yourself in your position of authority. Successful business people achieve their success using many different managerial styles. I have seen a few of the different management styles and have practiced both the good as well as the bad in my leadership roles.

I admit I have been an arrogant, quick tempered and less than hospitable person when dealing with employees and colleagues in the past. It is not something that I am proud of. However, these experiences gave me insight into how not to act and in return gave me direction on how to be a better and more efficient business leader. Going about your daily routines and acting in an unprofessional matter only leads to internal strife and, in the end, decreased productivity.

Some managers come in like a tornado, screaming, yelling, throwing things and behaving in ways that may have been the norm in the past. This behavior is learned either from their experience with an old manager's style or they were actually taught this method by upper management. Some employees respond and work well with this management style. Thankfully, I was never employed by such a manager and have never practiced this style of leadership. My error was that I was not helpful or instructional in my ways of managing. My thought was that an employee should know what to do without my explaining it. This led to me not setting the example by explaining properly what the duties were. You need to lead by example and manage a group by knowing and understand every part of the work that is taking place.

There are also managers out there that are just money grubbers, doing whatever it takes to get the largest amount of cash in their pocket. Greed is their focus and they will manipulate, lie, cheat or use any other tactic that will deliver the cash. When I worked for a mortgage lender near the end of the mortgage boom our main job became that of fraud detectives. We worked with state auditors to help identify people that were involved in shady loan activity. Combing through files to catch their schemes to get loans approved and funded became part of our daily routine. After compiling a list of their fraudulent tricks it became easier to spot the shady loans that were coming through the pipeline. Still, the scams these dishonest people ran were ingenious in the ways they deceived investors. In the end, though, it all catches up with people who try to manipulate the system. If these people would just work as hard at legitimate business as they do to defraud they would all be millionaires.

Usually the people involved with the illegal and deceptive activities were individuals that had associated themselves with some manager or mastermind that implemented the schemes. Most of the time they were in groups that worked as teams to try to defraud any unsuspecting business that was not aware to their activities. You could usually follow the trail and expose more than one person once you were on to their financial scams.

On occasion, my wife has business meetings at seminars or conventions within her industry. She dreads the after meeting functions that almost always involve a night on the town, or more specifically, a night at a bar. Contacts are made and deals are struck at these gatherings but you also get the drunkards that come out and cause trouble. People may not intend to drink over their limit but it happens, and over-indulging usually leads to regret the next day. My wife recalls one instance when a person got a little too inebriated, made a fool out of himself and was fired when he returned to the home office. I have always called my wife the one drink wonder. She will usually have one drink, and that is her limit. At these functions, however, she chooses to have a soft drink with drink swizzle or umbrella instead of carrying on with the others

Self-control is an important component of being a successful manager or leader in any line of work. You will never lose when you approach with kindness, self-control and sensible thinking. At one time, my biggest issue as the company leader was losing my temper if I thought I was being slighted in a business deal. Once, I had a disagreement with a vendor over a bill. I thought I was right and there was no way this vendor was going to rip me off. "How dare you!" was the approach I took and I got on the phone to track down the culprits that created this injustice. Of course, the first person to pick up the phone would be some poor soul that did not know what I was talking about which enraged me even more. I demanded to speak with the head of operations on the phone. As soon as he was on the line I started the yelling like I was going off the rails of the crazy train. Then the worst thing happened. The guy on the other end was nice, easy going, calm and soft-spoken. He won. He defused the situation and slowly talked me down out of the tree. I got his point.

Clearly, this guy had experience and was practiced in handling difficult situations. He had the knowledge and training to resolve the matter at hand. This was not the only occasion I came off as the out of control crazy person and the controlled, sensible, rational and probably Christian way of thinking on the other end of the line controlled the outcome. This experience taught me a lesson on how to act that was given down through the Gospel.

> **Proverbs 29:23** A person's pride will humble him, but a humble spirit will gain honor.

My only academic regret is not going to law school. A law degree would have been a valuable addition to my business and working career over the years. There have been times I have lost an advantage to attorneys because of their understanding of the legal system. They did not have better knowledge or ability to work the case but they knew the legal procedures to resolve the issue. Knowledge of the court system is how legal representation serves the client in a legal situation or dispute. Having a law degree does not necessarily mean you have to be involved with court cases or trial work but it can open doors in other areas you pursue.

> **Proverbs 14:23** There is profit in all hard work, but endless talk leads only to poverty.

> **Proverbs 12:11** The one who works his land will have plenty of food, but whoever chases fantasies lacks sense.

4

God's Money

> **Matthew 6:19-21** ¹⁹Don't collect for yourselves treasures on earth, where moth and rust destroy and where thieves break in and steal. ²⁰But collect for yourselves treasures in heaven, where neither moth nor rust destroys, and where thieves don't break in and steal. ²¹For where your treasure is, there your heart will be also.

God has no use or need for money. What would God need a pocket full of cash for? Everything in the world that was, is or is about to be is His creation. We all have heard of the "Pearly Gates." That is just a small glimpse of how Heaven is described as the everlasting paradise. The streets are paved with gold and every kind of precious stone decorates the foundations of city. Everything from jasper, sapphire, chalcedony, emerald, sardonyx, carnelian, chrysolite, beryl, topaz, chrysoprase, jacinth, and amethyst decorate God's new world that awaits everyone who walks in His Word. If He can create this magnificent place there will never be a need to get a loan to build this paradise.

Possessions and money are created things that have been part of our lives since the beginning of time. God gave them to help us not only for personal use but to help with our system of trading with others. Throughout time there has been good uses and bad uses of these items. As mentioned before, God has never had any use for such things since they are all His and he created everything. Unfortunately, though, you just can't walk into a store and go "I am a Christian and God said I could put these shoes on His tab." The security guard would be quick on the scene to stop any attempt of walking out without paying for your item.

When Jesus arrived on the scene it is easy to notice that there was no need for money in our new Savior's life. Throughout the New Testament you find rules and procedures dedicated to the treatment and use of money. It is clear that obtaining and worrying about money was not on the priority list for Jesus. When Pharisees were trying to trip Him up about taxes to see if he was exempt from paying he simply had them go over to the water, pull out a fish, and take the needed tariff from its mouth.

> **Matthew 17:27** But, so we don't offend them, go to the sea, cast in a fishhook, and catch the first fish that comes up. When you open its mouth you'll find a coin. Take it and give it to them for Me and you.

The best, and most telling, example of the insignificance of money was that Judas Iscariot, the devil's henchman, and one of Jesus's twelve disciples, was in charge of the group's moneybag. God knew from the beginning that Judas was controlled by the devil and was going to betray Jesus in accordance with the scripture. It was even stated that he would help himself to the money without the knowledge of the others. In the end, he sold the life of Jesus for 30 silver coins. This gives a lot of insight to what money really means to our Lord and can happen if it controls our lives.

> **John 12:4-6** ⁴Then one of His disciples, Judas Iscariot (who was about to betray him), said, ⁵"Why wasn't this fragrant oil sold for 300 denarii and given to the poor?" ⁶He didn't say this because he cared about the poor but because he was a thief. He was in charge of the money bag and would steal part of what was put in it.

By putting your mind and focus on God all concerns or worries will be taken care of. If you put money ahead of the word of God it will lead to destruction, not only with your chance of having everlasting life but also your immediate needs and living here on earth. Money is a worthless part of genuine living but how you manage it can determine how your life on earth will carry out. Although, "worthless" is a counterintuitive description of money since we have to know its earthly value and use it in our modern existence. Money is used every day to purchase the necessities we need as humans living on God's earth.

> **Matthew 6:24** No one can be a slave of two masters, since either he will hate one and love the other, or be devoted to one and despise the other. You cannot be slaves of God and of money.

Of course we need to have money and manage it in our lives. God does not drop money down from heaven to provide for our earthly needs. He gives you instructions on how to deal with money in your life that can be applied and followed to help provide for your needs. Is this a guarantee that you are going to be wealthy and leave an inheritance to your children and grandchildren? That depends on how you live as a Christian and follower of our Lord and Savior Jesus. Money and finances are just a sidebar to the real issue, which is God's plan to have us with Him forever. Managed well, money is a tool to help promote the plans of God. How you use money will show the big picture of how you accept the Gospel in your life.

Looking at the educational system in the United States over the past 50 years we have seen a significant increase in people obtaining college degrees. Before that time success and large acquisitions of wealth were based on hard work and ingenuity. The ladder of success did not necessarily start with a diploma but by using knowledge and wisdom to pave your own way to success. Today, you have a lot of people relying on their piece of paper to pave their way and grant them instant wealth and success. But until you get out in the workforce, roll up your sleeves and put your plow to the field you have not proved your value in the workplace. I have known many individuals with master's degrees that could not get or hold a job. An advanced degree beyond a four-year program should not entitle you to the best jobs available. Certainly it can help to open some doors but until you have worked and proved yourself you are just holding a piece of paper.

I am not putting down education beyond the undergraduate level but I am stating that you should not expect to garner the rewards of work right out of the gate just because you have a master's degree. My wife and I both received bachelor's degrees and I am glad I married someone I can share my educational experience with. The degrees we obtained probably would not be high on a recruiter's list. My wife earned an art degree and although she is a great artist she realized that the starving artist route was not what she wanted. She was fortunate to have a friend that recommended a job in the insurance industry. It was not something she thought she would ever be involved in but she walked off the stage with her diploma and into an interview with a hiring manager. They met at a restaurant and he gave her a map and AAA membership for travel and hired her on the spot.

My route to college graduation is a little more unconventional than my wife's. After three and half years on campus I went to a counselor for some guidance. I had been taking a lot of business classes along with geography courses, which was my field of interest. Geography is related to almost any subject or specialty field you can study. Whether demographics, territorial or topography, geography connects to just about any subject. After speaking with the counselor I found the route I could take, Bachelor of General Studies. Being a student at the University of Kentucky I had never heard of the degree. After asking around, and getting a few laughs along the way, I was told I would be receiving the BGS, or affectionately called the BlueGrass Special. This was a long hidden—you have done your time, did fairly well in class, played ball during your eligibility on campus, its been a good time—degree. My BGS hangs upon my wall showing the accomplishment of five years on campus with the minimum number of hours needed to graduate.

Now I had my degree and I was ready to walk in to the first job interview and demand X salary and my desk with a window view. I learned quickly that my BGS degree was really not as impressive as the students back on campus cracked it up it to be. After coming back to my hometown I realized that the smaller market city would not have anything to offer me so I started to look at other options.

A friend of mine had moved to California a few years out of high school. He had tried a couple of years of college but was not suited for academia as he was more of an entrepreneurial-minded person. This guy had worked since he was 15 and even bought his first car and paid for all his expenses while in high school. Of the many jobs he had the one that honed his skills and salesmanship was that of a door-to-door vacuum salesman. He even came up to the campus where I attended college and stayed for a few months to canvas the area. I went out a few times with him to assist and observe this process that, if successful, could result in some big paydays.

Anyone who wants to go into sales should apprentice in a door-to-door program like the one my friend was in. You will find out quickly if you are up to the challenge of being a salesman. Do you have what it takes to knock on the door, get a foot inside and make the money by closing the deal? Many people say, "I can't do sales," or "sales is not for me." I believe this wholeheartedly because it is a hard road if you are not cut out for the task. To walk up to a door in a cold call mode takes a personality that is not afraid of a challenge, to say the least. Getting inside and doing a presentation of a product that someone may or may not have or want is what develops the salesman's abilities.

I can remember my friend and I going up to a door and watching him KNOCK. A person answers and my friend gets out a "Hel...," then the resident says, "Go away we don't need anything," slam. My friend then gives another KNOCK, KNOCK. Again a quick opening of the door, and my friend goes, "Hello, can I...," then the resident says "I TOLD YOU WE DON'T NEED ANYTHING," and a louder slam follows. My friend then goes into round three, KNOCK, KNOCK, KNOCK. By now I am starting to express my concerns that this man might open the door the third time with a gun but on this day the third time must have been the charm. After opening the door a third time my friend got his sales spiel started and got in the door for a presentation. After an hour or so the customer had signed the papers and was the proud owner of an eighteen hundred dollar vacuum that, with attachments included, did 57 different things around the home not limited to painting, unclogging your sink and cutting your hair.

Every job requires unique skills that we may or may not have. The Lord can nurture your abilities and give you the knowledge and wisdom to excel in whatever field you pursue. However, if you are not working for the good of His Kingdom it is all for naught. If you work for your desires and not His glory any success you may have will be short lived and in the end you will be destined to fail. God wants us to win, succeed and do well in whatever we attempt but He also wants us to honor Him. The quickest, easiest, and the most commonly used way monetarily is by our tithe.

If your career path is sales you should learn to cold call, just to see if this is your line of work. You will learn a lot of life lessons during this time, many of which correlate with the word of the gospel. There is a lot of humbleness, perseverance, humility and patience required to be a successful salesperson. God equips you all with these attributes but you have to practice them in all aspects of your life. To be successful and take care of your family takes a variety of skills all working in unison. The more you incorporate these skills into your total package the benefits you reap will follow.

Colossians 3:23-25 [23]Whatever you do, do it enthusiastically, as something done for the Lord and not for men, [24]knowing that you will receive the reward of an inheritance from the Lord—you serve the Lord Christ. [25]For the wrongdoer will be paid back for whatever wrong he has done, and there is no favoritism.

All along your career path there will be times you feel violated or mistreated in the workplace. In most cases you are going to have a legitimate grievance associated with the circumstances.

The human factor is bound to create conflicts that work against the goals you want to achieve. How we handle such situations is the key to succeeding at what we are trying to accomplish. Continuously confronting issues or problems that arise and finding amicable solutions is the only way to resolve workplace problems. Sitting around and stewing about it, only invites the devil to get a foothold in the situation. That his is job: to disrupt the workplace and bring everyone down.

> **Ephesians 4:26-32** [26]Be angry and do not sin. Don't let the sun go down on your anger, [27]and don't give the Devil an opportunity. [28]The thief must no longer steal. Instead, he must do honest work with his own hands, so that he has something to share with anyone in need. [29]No rotten talk should come from your mouth, but only what is good for the building up of someone in need, in order to give grace to those who hear. [30]And don't grieve God's Holy Spirit, who sealed you for the day of redemption. [31]All bitterness, anger and wrath, insult and slander must be removed from you, along with all wickedness. [32]And be kind and compassionate to one another, forgiving one another, just as God also forgave you in Christ.

I have been in many work environments where the tension makes life miserable for everyone. People talking about each other behind the backs of their coworkers and forming alliances splits the team in half and leads to decreased productivity. This kind of environment is a road to failure if not addressed and corrected. If it cannot be corrected I would recommend cutting the ties and moving on to the next job. If you are doing your best but the work environment is not allowing you to succeed it is time to start looking for another opportunity. Over the years I have heard many people say, "I hate my job." Remember that you are in control of your situation and if your job is not working out for you pack it up and find something else. It might not be the next week, next month or year but if you stick with it you will find another opportunity.

One word of caution I would like to also offer is to keep your current job while you are looking for something else. It is always easier to move into a new job from your existing employment without any down time in between. I have made the mistake of quitting a job without anything in the works. This can lead to a very bad situation if the time between jobs drags on without any income. Don't take this chance if at all possible.

> **Proverbs 10:17** The one who follows instruction is on the path to life, but the one who rejects correction goes astray.

However, if there is always conflict and strife in the workplace take a good look in the mirror and make sure you are conducting yourself as a model employee or business owner. Check yourself, because you might be the problem in the work environment. Some people cannot take instruction without pushing back. These people are going to argue and fight because they always have to be right. If this is you, the person in charge is going to eventually terminate the employment arrangement.

Everyone needs to work together and strive for the same goals. When the team is on the same path work will be a lot less hectic and may even be pleasant. In small business, especially, there needs to be complete unity to reach your objectives. A house divided cannot stand and sooner or later will fail.

Working together as a team and being on the same page makes for a productive workforce.

This is one reason I have been mostly involved in team sports as a player and coach. I knew growing up and playing that I have a position and spot on the field that is my area and I have to work and play hard to secure my spot on the field. If I am successful at my position I will be doing my part on the team. I try to inject this concept into every team I coach. By letting the players know they have a duty and role within the team and it is their responsibility to uphold their position it gives them an important job to accomplish. I also let them know that this is a lesson and they will be called upon to fulfill their assignments not only at work but in life.

> **Proverbs 27:17** Iron sharpens iron, and one man sharpens another.

5

Different Paths to Success

Romans 12:6-8 [6]According to the grace given to us, we have different gifts: If prophecy, use it according to the standard of faith; [7]if service, in service; if teaching, in teaching; [8]if exhorting, in exhortation; giving, with generosity; leading, with diligence; showing mercy, with cheerfulness.

A friend once approached me with a new self-help book—one of those good relative, bad relative publications detailing how to approach finances and living. I read the first couple of pages and handed it back to him. The book was basically his life as it applied to money and working. I had known this friend since my early teens. He was an athlete who balanced his ball playing with part time jobs in high school. In college he played baseball but he realized that a professional career was a distant dream. He decided to start focusing on getting his degree while at the same time working full time to pay for his education.

This man, in his early twenties held a full time job, had his own place to live and carried a full time class load. In today's world it is rare to carry such a load at a young age but in earlier days this was more common. Today, people do no put in the extra effort to support themselves at this age. We should get back to the work ethic that builds character and life skills to carry us through life.

Today, my friend has worked his way up to a corporate management position with the same company he worked for while in school. He has moved from his first home to a nicer house in a newer part of town. When I helped him get his home out of construction financing into permanent financing he had one of the highest credit scores I had ever seen. I am sure that has not changed and I could almost guarantee that his current financials include only a home mortgage that will be paid off soon.

Soon after our kids arrived, my wife and I set up a trust with instructions for our finances and assets. When the attorney asked who would be the trustee if anything happened to us it was easy to arrive at a decision. My old friend's proven track record of long-term stability and financial success made it easy for both of us to appoint him trustee. Whatever instructions we put in the forms would be handled correctly and efficiently by the man who was his own self-help book.

> **Proverbs 13:7** One man pretends to be rich but has nothing; another pretends to be poor but has great wealth.

Some people have a "look at me, look at me" attitude towards their lives. They have to have the high dollar clothing, drive the high-end cars and are always trying to impress. I am not against nice clothes, nice cars or nice things but when it is all people talk about it becomes pretentious. It has never made sense to me to pay $80 for a shirt just because it has a logo when you can buy the same shirt for $20 without the logo. Why would I pay four times the cost to be free advertising for a huge manufacturer?

I have known a lot of people that live the flash lifestyle. You see all the "bling," cars, fancy clothes and other extras they believe bring status. Secretly, though, they are in debt up to their turned up collar. The life of continuously trying to impress the neighbor is to no avail. Yes, you have to dress for success when dealing with clients and working in a professional environment. This can be done, though, buy driving a clean nice car in the $20,000 range. There is no need to buy a $70,000 vehicle. If you are a millionaire and have the cash to buy the $70k car, go for it but even when you have the money I still do not see the need.

> **Proverbs 29:5** A man who flatters his neighbor spreads a net for his feet.

Smart people do not care what they drive or what they wear. They are not wearing rags but they are not wearing the $200 shirts or $500 shoes either. Smart people have cash and don't care what the person next to them thinks. They have worked hard and accumulated wealth and don't want to blow it on frivolous purchases. People pretending to have cash seem to talk about it all the time and money is their main focus. The quest to accumulate cash and riches only leads to their downfall. They believe if only they have this or that and acquire enough money it will be all that they need to be happy.

Usually, in their greed to obtain their riches materialistic people lose touch with what really matters in life. Wealth is not bad, but if you become a slave to the love of money it will not work out for you in the end. Our ultimate goal is to dwell in the kingdom of the Lord and if you think the path lies in your riches you are definitely on the wrong road. Many nice people have worked honestly and made a good living but if they think wealth is all that matters they lose sight of what really matters which is everlasting life.

> **Luke 18:18-24** [18]A ruler asked Him, "Good Teacher, what must I do to inherit eternal life?" [19]"Why do you call Me good?" Jesus asked him. "No one is good but One—God. [20]You know the commandments: Do not commit adultery; do not murder; do not steal; do not bear false witness; honor your father and mother." [21]"I have kept all these from my youth," he said. [22]When Jesus heard this, he told him, "You still lack one thing, sell all that you have and distribute it to the poor, and you will have treasure in heaven. Then come, follow me." [23]After he heard this, he became extremely sad, because he was very rich. [24]Seeing that he became sad, Jesus said, "How hard it is for those who have wealth to enter the kingdom of God! [25]For it is easier for a camel to go through the eye of a needle than for a rich person to enter the kingdom of God."

There are others who are simply corrupt when it comes to their wealth. Dishonest or crooked individuals who conduct their business in a way that takes advantage of people in the process. Through deception or misrepresentation they will aim to make the maximum off every customer or client. A good example is the interest that might be charged in a business transaction. Usually, when interest is involved there is a range that can be presented and, of course, the higher the rate the higher the lender's profits. The lender will work for the higher rate even if it is not the best option for the client.

> **Proverbs 28:8** Whoever increases wealth through excessive interest collects it for the one who is kind to the poor.

The largest credit that you will ever apply for will be to purchase your home. This should also be the only credit that you ever hold as a debt. Every other form of credit is unnecessary and should never be used. Why would you ever need a credit card or credit line? The concept of credit really does not make sense. Purchasing with credit says "I want this but I don't want to pay for it right now." Does this make sense? Once you take your purchase home it loses value and it is not paid for. Also, while paying for it you are going to pay interest on top of the original cost. Would you go to a shop and say "I want to buy this $100 item but may I please pay you $125?" Not a smart way to use your money.

Whatever work you get into make sure you approach it with all you've got and success will follow you in your aspirations. In coaching youth league ball I let all the kids know at the beginning of the season what I expect. There is only rule that relates to hitting the field and that is to give it all you've got. I get loud sometimes but it is only going to be when you are not hustling and giving your best. If you are not out there to play and give 100% you are not only hurting the team but also letting yourself down. Considering the ages of some of the young players it is not only the effort but also a safety issue. In football if you are just going half speed and not paying attention someone is going to let you know it by decleating you as you stand around with your guard down. The same thing with baseball, if you are standing around not paying attention to what is going on during play a batter can rip a ball and hit you right in the head. It is not fun on the field in either situation when these things happen. Then as a whole if you have another team that is giving more effort and hustle they are going to be the ones that come out on top.

Proverbs 11:28 Anyone trusting in his riches will fall, but the righteous will flourish like foliage.

6

Hard Work

> **Proverbs 6:10-11** ¹⁰A little sleep, a little slumber, a little folding of the arms to rest, ¹¹and your poverty will come like a robber, your need, like a bandit.

In recent years the United States, as a whole, is getting out hustled and out worked by people that are willing to put in the effort to get ahead. I know people who have come to the United States from other countries and have built successful businesses. When people are not scared to put in a hard days work each and every day there is going to be reward at the end. My neighbor from the Middle East started out waiting tables in a hotel chain in Los Angeles. He came to Nashville to check out a large hotel with a large convention facility. After interviewing he was offered a job on the spot, starting that day.

Soon, he was in Nashville waiting tables at the large convention complex. He began to network and came upon an opportunity to buy a convenience market. He and his brother scraped some money together and made the purchase. Working alternate 12-hour shifts my neighbor and his brother got the business going in the right direction. This became his first successful business and today he now owns over 20 convenience and self-service gas stations throughout the city. Also, he has acquired real estate and apartment buildings in his home country. My neighbor is a true success story of someone who worked hard and gave it his all.

The construction business is an area where I have seen Hispanic people become highly successful. One man has shown me, not only with hard work but also with faith in the Lord, what can be accomplished. Growing up in Central America, this man would get up at 3:00 a.m. to walk the cow and buggy to pick up the sugar cane then would go back home to go to school. He lived in a house with dirt floors, no running water and an outhouse. This man is under the age of 40 so we are not talking about days of long ago. Eventually, he made his way to the United States and worked long hours to survive.

When I met him I was in the process of building a house and he was referred to me for doing some roof work. He did not have a crew or help and performed all the work himself. He hand carried 350 bundles of shingles onto the roof and did an outstanding job on the completion of the roof. He did not have reliable transportation, so when time came to settle up for the work he had done, he requested that I purchase a truck he had found so he could continue his work in the construction field.

I was impressed with his ability to complete any task. I was expanding a commercial piece of property by adding 4,400 square feet. It was in an area with small lots where adjacent properties were within a few feet of each other. Built in the 1950s, this place had established trees over 50 feet tall. I did not want to spend thousands on a professional tree service because I was not sure they could perform the job in such a tight space. I showed my friend what needed to be done and he said he could take care of it for me. He proceeded to get a small chain saw, scale the trees and cut them from the top down.

As I watched him work I was amazed. Here was a man

hanging onto six inch limbs, swaying back an forth, leaning out with one hand and cutting huge limbs one by one. To make it even more difficult, he had to engineer a system of ropes to lower the limbs so they would not land on any cars or adjacent properties. After witnessing this man's impressive "do anything attitude" I hired him to do anything that came up around the office or home. For a while, I kept him on a 40-hours a week schedule. A person who is willing to work, and is unafraid to attempt a job becomes a valuable asset.

When I ran out of work for my friend we did not communicate much for a period of time. Recently, I needed some painting done on some high spots around the outside trim of our house. I knew whom to call, so I rang my friend and he made it over to do the small job. I asked him how business was going and he said he was staying busy. In fact, he had 11 employees with all the work that he had to complete. I was glad for him and happy to see someone that had been through such a hard life become successful.

> **Proverbs 16:3** Commit your activities to the Lord and your plans will be achieved.

I believe that if you are working in a way that does not honor the Lord you are working in futility. Even though you might see some success from the fruits of your labor it will not last. When working you must keep focus on what is most important, your Lord and Savior, who gave you the ability and knowledge to succeed and is in charge of all that is. If you just accumulate as much as possible and store up the money for your own desires what good will you achieve? Do not be caught up in our earthly world that has no eternal value.

Recently in the news there has been a huge controversy

over the contributions of Chick-fil-A. Chick-fil-A was built by a Christian family that has followed the rules of God and His word and as a result have created a successful business. They followed all of the elements I have spoken about in this book and we can easily see how God has blessed the work of their hands.

> **Proverbs 11:24** One person gives freely, yet gains more: another withholds what is right only to become poor.

With the success of the company, Chick-fil-A has been given the opportunity to give back by contributing to many different organizations and programs. Recently, my son attended a football camp where Chick-fil-A was one of the sponsors. They helped fund a camp T-shirt, a certificate of achievement award and on the last day of camp the cow mascot showed up and every camper was given a free chicken sandwich coupon. Our family has gotten to know the local marketing representative that markets their stores and she is always working hard to promote local involvement with their locations. During the school year they have student nights with a designated night for each school in the area. It is always a great time for the kids to get out and socialize outside the school setting with their friends. It is our kids' favorite place to eat and we do not mind waiting in the usually longer lines to support a company that gives so much back.

Chick-fil-A's giving has been in the news recently and has brought division in some areas of the country. Some people are outraged that some of the beneficiaries of the generous contributions by Chick-fil-A have been Christian organizations. One organization in particular promotes family values and practices. Chick-fil-A is a successful business with spiritual owners who live by biblical standards and follow the word of the Lord. They choose to donate and contribute their money to an entity that works to strengthen the concept of the family and, in return, are attacked for their generous actions.

I stand with the owners of Chick-fil-A and follow the same moral values as laid out for us in the gospel. This book is not intended to function as the morality compass for me to tell anybody else how to act or think. You will have to determine and make that call on you own. But one thing I will do is recommend you read the Bible and understand what the gospel is saying. You will have a much better understanding of events that occur in your daily living and a good measure to what is right and wrong. Does this make the owners of Chick-fil-A or me a bigot because we follow what the Bible says? Of course not. Will the owners of Chick-fil-A or I go out and protest and march against the gay movements around the country? Of course not. I am amazed at how the mayors of two major cities can jump on a band wagon to oppose a company that has done nothing more than support a Christian organization. You would think the agendas of large cities would be full, but in a never ending election campaign there has to be a cause that caters to some of the voters.

I do not believe in or condone the practices of gay couples. But it is not up to me to judge anyone. I try to follow the number rule God puts in our daily living and that is to love. While I may not agree with some people I am still called to love you as God has instructed. The time and energy it takes to hate can easily be turned towards love and the results are a lot more pleasant.

> **John 13:34** I give you a new commandment: love one another. Just as I have loved you, you must also love one another.

We will continue to dine at one of the best food establishments in our area, not only for the food, service and opportunity to patronize a great company, but also because the owners stand for what is right and honor the Lord. Our children say Chick-fil-A is their favorite place because they love the Lord.

> **Luke 6:37-38** ³⁷Do not judge, and you will not be judged. Do Not condemn, and you will not be condemned. Forgive, and you will be forgiven. ³⁸Give, and it will be given to you; a good measure- pressed down, shaken together, and running over will be poured into you lap. For with the measure you use, it will be measured back to you.

Hard work does not only apply to employment. There are a number of other activities that you will have to apply the skill of hard work to accomplish a favorable outcome. Some important areas where hard work takes place is in our relationships with our spouses, children, co-workers and neighbors. A lot of times it takes going beyond the basic work assignment to build a successful relationship with one of these people. There are a lot of relationships that require a little more effort to get to a point where it creates a pleasant and peaceful outcome.

I have noticed my wife over the years in the way she always goes beyond the normal levels of kindness. She practices a kind approach with just about everyone she comes into contact with and most of the time the effort produces a pleasant experience for everyone. She has the ability to make people happy when briefly crossing paths at places like a fast food restaurant, grocery checkout line or a variety of other places that involve interactions with strangers. I have seen people in store aisles stop and divulge information that I bet immediate family members are not privy. She is just one of those individuals people like to talk to and tell their life story.

Recently we were at a fast food restaurant with the kids and while at the counter the worker and my wife were carrying on like they knew each other for years. The kids asked why do people always want to talk to you? My wife told them that she really cared what was going on with people, was truly interested and that it was a lot easier to be nice. Then the kids told me, "Yeah dad you just go—here is my money, give me my food, don't talk to me and hurry up." Now if someone talks to me and is being nice and friendly I am always just as nice back. But most of the time I am just indifferent and do not work at extending the olive branch or initiating the kindness. I guess I have been one of those that considered it to be effort that I did not want to put forth. I was one that did not work hard to establish a friendly interaction and did not take advantage of an opportunity to deliver a kind word or gesture.

When you have a positive attitude and friendly disposition I have noticed that in every situation it makes you and the other person strive to reciprocate the actions that take place. I am striving to become more like my wife when dealing with people and make every encounter a positive one. If you have the attitude of it is way easier to be nice why would you not want to practice this all of the time?

I had a confrontation with a neighbor that could have gone in the wrong direction if I had not taken the scripture of loving your neighbor and praying for your enemy. Most neighborhoods have one or two residents who stir up trouble instead of being neighborly and working out any problems that come along. In our neighborhood there is one family that I would consider the best "homeowners" in the community. They have a very nice house that they maintain immaculately, very polite, respectful children, and dogs that are well controlled and never outside the yard. My family, on the other hand, has a less than manicured yard and our dog sometimes breaks lose and cruises the neighborhood. We finally got him contained by putting a solar powered, low voltage hot wire at the bottom of our fence to keep him inside our yard. Even with a completely hot-wired perimeter, though, there are still times when he makes his escape.

One day, our dog made an escape and headed down to another house in the neighborhood where there is a dog that our dog likes to play with. On this particular day, a resident took offense at the unscheduled doggy play date and tried to find out why a dog was running loose. She happened upon a neighbor that we really do not know well and have not been friendly with. The woman of the family was involved with the neighborhood association and we had some minor bylaw issues related to construction. There has been some animosity between our families.

This neighbor was listening to this person complain about our dog. Everyone knows our dog is very friendly and playful. The worst thing he might do is jump on you wanting a hug or use your plants as a fire hydrant. That said, I do not blame anyone for being irritated that my dog has gotten lose and is using the bathroom in their yard and breaking the association rules running loose. My neighbor finally got irritated enough that he threw our dog in the back of his car and brought the dog home to confront the problem on our front steps.

He quickly told me what had happened and continued by saying he would like to put a "blanking" bullet in our dog's head. I apologized for my dog getting out and I would try to not let it happen again. I do not want my dog, that I am responsible for, causing disturbances. After the neighbor left I started to think how aggressively and un-neighborly he behaved in the whole situation. Then I started to get mad and think of all the many different ways it could have been handled. But then I thought about how we have never had any relationship with this family and to them we might seem to be just as bad a neighbor.

After speaking with my wife she had a simple response to

the whole situation and just said, "Pray about it." That was her plan of action with the former boss that was attacking her with the lawsuit and it should be my plan of action too. I do not want to get in a fight in my own neighborhood. Besides, I am sure it would violate some form of covenant within our HOA bylaws.

Within a few days and a few prayer requests later there was another jailbreak by our socially deprived dog. Of course with the recent incident, and us not wanting our dog to be loose in the first place, a posse was assembled for the quick capture of our third child. First, I went to the neighbor who has three dogs and considers our dog her fourth friend. I visited with her for a while and she assured me my dog was close by as she knew his routine from his many visits. After a considerable amount of time waiting I just said I better start the neighborhood patrol to see if I could spot him and get him back home. After making a couple passes through our community I came across the man with the bounty on our dog's head. He was just standing out in the driveway staring in my direction. I knew something was about to happen and it was limited to only a few outcomes.

I stop my truck in front of his house, walk around to the other side and ask him if he has seen our dog. He answers no, but the dog has been there and he points at a pile of dog doody. I tell him if it my dog's I will get it if he has some towels or rags available. He says no big deal and not to worry about it. We then start to talk and, to my surprise, he could not have been any friendlier. He began to joke, laugh and smile and carry on like the friendly neighbors we should be. I was taken back by the whole event just because this was a guy we had not really spoken to since moving into our small neighborhood.

I do not know if we had always met each other on bad days or had just never reached out and been friendly. I know I could have been more cordial. Whatever the reason, I do believe that the praying created a more favorable outcome. We probably will not be planning a vacation with our two families but hopefully now we can at least be the friends and neighbors the Lord wants us to be. Someone you may perceive to be your enemy has all the promise to be a friend, all one has to do is extend the olive branch. I think you will be amazed at what kind of response is waiting at the other end of the offering.

> Mark 12:29-31 [29]"This is the most important," Jesus answered: Listen, Israel! The Lord our God, the Lord is One. [30]Love the Lord your God with all your heart, with all your soul, with all your mind, and with all your strength. [31]"The second is: Love your neighbor as yourself. There is no other commandment greater than those."

7

Need a Hired Hand

> **Proverbs 13:11** Wealth obtained by fraud will dwindle, but whoever earns it through labor will multiply it.

Over your lifetime you will make countless payments for services rendered to complete a job that you are not qualified to perform. Some trade services include plumbers, electricians, auto mechanics or HVAC repairmen. The professional services involved in the purchase of a house include realtors, mortgage loan officers and title closing agents. You also have doctors, attorneys, accountants, insurance agents and a long list of similar professions that require specialized training to perform.

Most of the professions and services mentioned above require some form of licensure. Before someone is licensed to perform these jobs a regulatory board certifies that the person has completed all the education required to do the job. This could involve extended classroom work along with testing to assure that the knowledge is in place to successfully perform the job. Also, most all professions require insurance or bonding to work in a given field. These jobs may carry a fair amount of risk and professionals should have coverage for themselves as well as their clients. When hiring a professional you need to be aware of any insurance requirements and make sure that policies are in place, especially for construction and liability for a health provider.

Given this information, I would like to add some insight based on my experiences in the construction and real estate businesses. I have been involved in a number of construction projects as well as the purchase and sale of many properties over the years. Just because someone has all the credentials does not mean they are qualified to do the job. There are a variety of services in the construction industry that will require a permit such as electrical, mechanical, plumbing, etc. You may also need to hire people for drywall, carpentry, paint, masonry or roofing. In some states these areas of expertise do not require a license. You might be hiring a "so-called" expert in one of these fields that does not have the experience to do the job.

Another hurdle is when you find the best carpenter, painter, or any other expert trade person but he doesn't know how to run his business. I have had people show up with good references but who don't have the organizational skills to complete a job. They will arrive at the job site, go around and evaluate the job and come up with a reasonable quote and time frame to complete the job. Then you get the story of how they just have to wrap up another job and they could get right over after that is completed to start your job. Would it be possible to get some of the money now and start your job next week? This is a big red flag in the construction industry. If a sub-contractor is playing catch up with their other jobs they need money now to finish a previous job. The whole business is a catch-up game that doesn't allow them to finish a job in a timely manner or within budget. It is a continuous cycle of looking for the next job to fund the previous one. Then, your unfinished job goes on the back burner with no foreseeable completion date.

Another bad sign is when the crew shows up with their lawn

chairs. Then you can count on slow work on a daily basis. On the other hand, if you see a crew show up with their own hot plates you can be certain you have a crew that is going to stay on site, eat a quick lunch and get back to work. I am a big fan of hot plates.

In some instances money does need to be paid up front. If you have a project that requires special or custom items such as tile, appliances, specialty roofing, etc. you may need to pay for those materials before the work begins. In these cases make sure you order, pay and pick up the product yourself and your hired workers will have what they need to complete the job. Unless your workers have a proven track record, do not front them the cash to get materials. This can lead to problems like unexpected delays, incomplete work, and the worse case scenario, which is they take off with your money.

Your house is the biggest purchase you will make in your life. For such a large expenditure you need to have several professionals involved in the transaction. You start with a real estate agent who looks for homes that meet your needs and desires. Real estate agents are licensed professionals who have completed a certain number of classroom hours and passed an exam. There are multiple requirements for real estate agents including insurance coverage, continuing education, association memberships and ethical guidelines established by the state. Principal brokers serve as the managing office where an agent would place his license. Even with all of these requirements in place, however, this does not mean that a real estate agent will be able to meet your needs.

Over the years I have worked with many real estate agents as a principal broker and the one major conclusion I can draw is that there is as wide a range of abilities as there are real estate agents. With a little time, money and common sense it is easy to qualify for a real estate license, but to excel as a real estate agent you need the "know-how" to conduct business in a way that best serves the client. As a consumer, you want to be assured you are putting your biggest investment into the hands of person who is competent in their knowledge of the real estate market. Make sure you have done your research and have enough reliable information to not only choose the right agent but to make sure you are making an informed choice in the purchase of your home.

When buying a home you are going to have a handful of other participants help evaluate and make sure your purchase is a reasonable and good choice. Unless you are paying cash for the home you will be getting a loan or mortgage. The lender is going to scrutinize the transaction to make sure the value of the property that is going to be the collateral on the promissory note is equal to the mortgage. An appraisal will make sure the home is actually worth the purchase price. This gives you some protection from buying a property that may be overpriced.

A title search is going to give a snapshot of the property's recorded boundaries, owners and any debt that may be attached to the property. This is a very important procedure that should accompany all real estate transactions. You think you have found the best property at the right price. Every external detail seems to make it your dream home but the title work could reveal a total mess with liens, disputed property lines, or other issues that can make it a less than desirable property.

A final step to give you some peace of mind about the home you are buying is to get a home inspection. In any contract you are presenting on a potential purchase you want to put in the body of the contract that the purchase is contingent on a home inspection. Do your research and find a reputable person that knows all the ins and outs of home construction. I have worked with a number of home inspectors over the years and there is a wide range of ability in this field of work, as in all businesses. I remember one guy hanging out for about an hour, walking around, looking at the roof and making other visual inspections. At the end he had nothing to say about the house then tells me this is just a part time gig and I should come by watch him play guitar with his band downtown. I've had other inspectors take half a day and even cover stuff like checking each burner of the stove to see if it is properly working. Which inspector do you want looking at your home?

I have seen people let the realtor for the person selling the house pick the inspector. If you let the seller control the process of the home inspection they are going to call the guitar man who is going to give the home a clean bill of occupancy. A good rule to follow is to control the process yourself and find an independent inspector who is going to work for you and you alone.

Another level of professionals are those people who have gone past the four years of undergraduate studies and mastered their trade with graduate programs, medical school or law school. These professionals invest a lot of time and money in their education that should, in the long run, produce a higher income. Even though someone has done their time in the classroom, obtained their degree and passed the testing boards it does not mean he is practicing proficiently in his given profession. I have over the years run into medical professionals, lawyers and other such professionals that have not lived up to the title on their door.

In today's academic environment there are more ways than ever to obtain a degree but the quality of that degree is diminishing. With degrees being handed out more frequently some people have made it through the system without the skills necessary to effectively practice their profession. I would not say these people are incompetent but they are not able to perform at an acceptable level. Someday, they might acquire the insight to perform to standard but it takes a lot of experience to master any vocation.

Being part of many businesses over the years I have seen both qualified and unqualified individuals in every field. Attorneys are a great example of how there can be wide range of abilities in a given profession. When dealing with very large firms you will find categories and groupings of attorneys that specialize in specific fields. These large attorney groups are very diverse and charge a premium based on their menu of specialized services. These groups need the large fees to cover the overhead required to operate the firm. There is a long list of support staff that assists the attorneys and they may need to be as specialized as the attorneys themselves. If you are in a situation that requires the knowledge of a specific area of the law by all means hire an expert in that field.

You can go up and down any business area in any town and see small offices dotting the landscape with Attorney at Law or Esq. on the doorway. Before you consult with one of these lawyers you should do a little homework. Make sure the attorney is well versed in the area of law in which you are needing counsel. Ask other people that have used the attorney for similar services. Do not ask other attorneys. I have found that a lot of attorneys are networked and will cover for each other's reputation. They may not be giving inaccurate information but they might not be delivering unbiased answers. The bottom line is that someone may be an attorney but it does not necessarily mean he can handle your specific situation.

The same can be said about some doctors I have encountered. Over the past decade our most distressing medical issues have involved our children. These situations occurred in emergencies that filled us with fear of the unknown. In these cases we went straight to the doctor to get immediate answers. These answers, I have noticed, vary depending on the medical professional you consult. It is really important to get second opinions and acquire all the information related to the diagnosis. Find out everything that is available to make sure you get the right answer. Caring for your health, not to mention the health of your loved ones, is the most important use of an outside professional that you will experience.

I am not trying to knock attorneys, doctors, construction professionals or any other profession. However, in every field of work there is the incompetence factor. Some people do not have the ability to carry out their duty because they are unwilling or just fall short on their ability. The overwhelming majority of people do an excellent job in their given profession. They truly take their jobs seriously and work to meet the standards of their clients. I am sure most of the people that do a poor job in their fields do not stay in business long. Do your homework and make sure you are hiring a professional that will meet your expectations.

If you are an athlete or entertainer you will require agents to negotiate on your behalf. It is important for you to do your homework as well. These people are working for you and are compensated based on your performance. In other words, they are getting a percentage of what they negotiate on your behalf. These people can be valuable assets for getting you more money and perks than you may have gotten on your own. When interviewing agents make sure you come in with "your team" to help advise you in the process. Have someone with you who has your interests at heart, not money. These industries involve a lot of money so you want to make the best choice. Here, the old adage "two heads are better than one" is a good rule to follow.

I recently saw a story about an all-star high school baseball prospect getting a contract right out of high school. In baseball, an over-the-top phenomenon will skip college and sign a major league contract out of high school. The scouts and major league team representatives have the advantage at this point because they know the procedures from working with many prospects over the years. For the player, it will be their first time to negotiate and sign a pro ball contract. Scouts will make low ball offers with quick payments thinking the young player will jump on any deal presented.

In above the story the young man's mom was involved in

the process and it became a whole different ball game. She had done her homework and the negotiations became a little more intense during the signing process. The team representative said it took a lot of work and many concessions for the final deal to be signed. This player had the best backer and top deal negotiator he could ever hope for: his mom.

An area that it is even harder to predict is the criminal or deceptive element in the workplace. Some people are just bad and look for opportunities to take advantage of people. They will scam, trick or defraud to get your money. It is not easy, but be diligent when choosing the person, group or firm to complete your work.

Proverbs 28:6 Better a poor man who lives with integrity than a rich man who distorts right and wrong.

Over the years I have known people who have had a considerable amount of cash. They did not appear to be wicked people. They seemed to be nice people working hard making a good living at what they do. But in a lot of cases one might not be aware of the underlying circumstances associated with someone you might know. I believe wholeheartedly that money earned by unjust ways or by means that are not up to God's standards will be quickly gone.

Proverbs 15:6 The house of the righteous has great wealth, but trouble accompanies the income of the wicked.

What if your wealth is obtained by legitimate means? There are many people that have worked hard and acquired large sums of money. You may be living well but with no knowledge of what really matters. You could just be hoarding money that was given through opportunities provided by God on your behalf. You might have worked hard to gain status or wealth but you cannot survive on your stockpile of cash without first honoring the Lord. We exist not in our own world but in the eternal life offered by God. There is not a monetary fee associated with what God has to offer us, we just need to rely on and honor His word.

> **Proverbs 11:4** Wealth is not profitable on a day of wrath, but righteousness rescues from death.

I once heard a man I met that had acquired millions over a very successful music and business career state, "I never hand over any of my hard earned money to someone else". He explained, "why does it make since just to hand over large amounts of cash to some individual or business that is looking to benefit off what I have made"? He added, "how do I know they are competent and proficient in their business transactions to secure and protect the money earned from my efforts?" All good questions to pose before you trust someone with your money.

Over the past recent years there has been brought to the public's attention all the so called Ponzi schemes that have been exposed. At the front of the schemes is a party that has set out to defraud and in return benefit from large amounts of cash investments. But with every fraudulent case there has to be the second party that involves an unsuspecting investor that is willing to hand over their money to the first party. I might not go as far as saying the blame for such a transaction is 50/50 but it comes close.

In most of the cases there is a hook to get an otherwise normal, hard working intelligent individuals to fork over their hard earned savings to a criminal. And usually it involves a concept or return on investment that is true good to be true. You will have the masterminds guaranteeing a return that is way above anything obtainable within the real business models. What then occurs is the element of greed and lack of commonsense from the people that fall for the schemes. You can tag these events with the statement "if something it too good to be true, it is". If the current market is offering rates of return in the 6% range and someone has a "no way you can lose" with a 20% return it will be a 100% guarantee that a scam is being played out.

There is always going to be a need for financial planners, tax advisors, accountants and other related advice associated with your finances. But again do your homework and make sure you are getting the proper advice and not releasing your hard earned money into the hands of the world of misappropriations. There has been and always will be someone out there trying to sell you the Eiffel Tower or Brooklyn Bridge. Just make sure you use the commonsense and wisdom that has been afforded you by the Lord.

> **Romans 16:17-18** [17]Now I implore you, brothers, watch out for those who cause dissensions and pitfalls contrary to the doctrine you have learned. Avoid them; [18]for such people do not serve our Lord Christ but their own appetites, and by smooth talk and flattering words they deceive the hearts of the unsuspecting.

8

You Wanna be a Rock Star

> **Romans 12:1-2** [1]Therefore, brothers, by the mercies of God, I urge you to present your bodies as a living sacrifice, holy and pleasing to God; this is your spiritual worshop. [2]Do not be confirmed to this age, but be transformed by the renewing of your mind, so that you may discern what is good, pleasing, and perfect will of God.

Sometimes our exceptional talents offer us the opportunity to make large amounts of cash. Maybe you play a mean guitar, have a voice that can fill a room, can hit a ball 450 feet or throw a 70-yard spiral down field on the mark. In these cases our talents can reward us with large amounts of money that exceeds most people's average income. How we handle such success reflects our relationship with the Lord. If these new found riches are not handled properly you can end up worse off than you were before the influx of cash.

Over the years I have known a lot of people at the top of the pay scale: professional athletes, successful businessman, musicians, entertainers, etc. and have seen the different financial outcomes of these individuals. People must have a deep understanding of how to treat money and how to handle the unusual circumstances associated with wealth. Without them, they are sure to fail in their financial journey and lose the success associated with their God given talents.

Playing ball at a young age I was around a lot of athletes. I never made it to the college level of sports but knew people with the ability to make it to that level. Once you make it to college ball you are playing on a semi-pro level that could be considered the minor leagues for professional play. In college, the most governed rule is that college players cannot accept gifts or money of any kind. If you follow college sports today you will see that the most frequent violation associated with schools and players is the acceptance of inappropriate gifts which violates college rules.

Although I did not play college ball I was fortunate enough to attend a premier university in one of, if not the best athletic conference in college sports. I grew up in the south and attended college there as well. I will also add the east to this geographic area and you can figure out on your own what conference I am talking about. If not, I will go ahead and tell you, the Southeastern Conference.

When I was in school in the eighties I saw what it was like to be an athlete at a large university. If you have the talent and ability to earn a scholarship it has a value that I am sure young athletes as well as parents take for granted. My first semester tuition cost $476 in the fall of 1983 and peaked at $627 a semester in the fall of 1987. The same education today costs ten times the price that I paid.

Another thing that has changed is the criteria to get into the university. With my entrance exams and grade point average I would never have made it into college based on the current standards. Even as a premier athlete there are minimums to qualify for acceptance into a university although they will not be scrutinized as if you were just a new student applying to attend school. If you have the gift to perform at this top level and in return get a college degree by all means make sure you get that degree. Athletes on campus are well taken care of. They have tutor labs, extra help in the form of guidance and a separate dining area for daily meals.

Getting that diploma should be first priority and in return it will stay with you for a lifetime. Most universities have corporate sponsors that supply large amounts of funding for the schools. In many cases they also assist student athletes with future employment. I saw many players after graduation get a job with a major backer of our school. Executives within companies that support a school are usually huge fans and know the players on all the teams. They are very supportive of the athletes and more than happy to offer them a job upon graduation or, in some cases, during the summers while still in school.

College level athletics have become a minor league training ground for professional sports. More and more student athletes leave early and go for the big money. That big money needs to be properly handled or it will be a harsh reality when you get to the end of your professional career. Careers are relatively short on average in the big three sports of football, baseball and basketball. On the average, pro careers last just 3.5 years in football, 5.5 years in baseball and just under 5 years in basketball. This means your career is done by the time you reach 30. Your life is just getting started and you need a plan B after the playing days are over.

Signing the big contract worth millions of dollars can be a mixed blessing. Most student athletes have had very little to live on during their college years. All of sudden there are no restraints on what they can do or purchase. Without education and preparation the large money can disappear as quickly as it arrived.

Based on today's 82 game schedules and a small roster of 12–15 players, the NBA has the highest per player salary with an average of around $5 million a year. I met an NBA player back in the '80s. I do not have the figures for the late '80s but a professional basketball player on average was still the highest paid athlete in the four main professional sports. It was a big moment for me just being around a pro athlete and talking about the pro life and what is was like to be at that level. It was my first time to actually be around some one my age that had hit millionaire status. I was just sitting at a table with him and a large amount of cocaine.

Personally I had never been a saint as I had done my share of drinking and smoking marijuana but the cocaine line, for a lack of a better term, was one I did not cross. Yes I tried it a couple of times but since I was one that had never drank coffee or drinks with any caffeine, the experience was way less than enjoyable. I guess it could be compared to drinking four pots of coffee with a chaser of multiple cans of the caffeine laced "energy drinks" that are available today. Add to it the anxiety associated with the feeling that your heart is about to explode or jump our of your chest and this is why I could never figure out why people would want to use cocaine.

I sat with the player while he snorted his lines and told me a sob story about when you get all this money everyone wants a piece of you. All I could think was, "Here is a man with a dream come true—an NBA contract making more than any other professional athlete and he is snorting cocaine, poisoning his body and mind." I didn't know if I should feel sorry for the guy or smack him for being so ignorant and doing drugs. He was about 6'10" and 240 pounds, which restrained me from throwing any punches. I never heard about him ever getting in trouble so hopefully he kicked this bad habit and finished out his basketball career on a happy note.

On another occasion I met a salesman who was personable, friendly and performed his job very well. My wife and I talked to the guy about topics other than the sale and when he told me his name I realized he had played in the Super Bowl a few years back. We were impressed enough by his personality and effectiveness as a salesperson that we offered to bring him into our business to see if it was something he might enjoy.

We did not hear from him for a while but he finally called and wanted to give it a shot. When he came to the office he was not driving nor did he have a car. He trained with us for a while but soon he left and we never heard back from him. During his short time with us he asked us to pull his credit report and see if he would qualify for a mortgage. His credit history showed the exact pattern from college to the pros then out of the pros. You could see a start with zero income to a spike of a big paycheck coming in and then back to zero in a short period of time. The drastic valley to peak to valley was all in relation to the NFL contract that he signed out of college.

Once he was on the roster there was a purchase of an $80,000 vehicle, accounts opened at high-end department stores and a second vehicle purchase all within a short time frame. Once the contract was terminated you could see the sharp decline in his financial situation. The vehicles were repossessed, the other accounts were either delinquent, closed or charged off and the once good credit rating was in ruins.

A recent report released on the ESPN show 30/30 stated that 78% of NFL players are bankrupt or in financial distress within two years of retirement. And an estimated 60% of NBA players are in the same situation within five years of retirement.

I learned a lot about the life of a professional football player from my short time working with this former Super Bowl starter. The NFL is one of the largest and most successful industries in the world. It is a business and in the world of business what is beneficial to the business may not be beneficial to the employee. The NFL has a players association that helps and assists players after retirement. The health benefits package being offered to players is a main topic of concern when the players are negotiating contracts. Health insurance is provided for a time based on certain criteria within current guidelines of the NFL players' agreements. Today, to be vested in the NFL you must have four years of service in the league. Based on recent stats the average tenure in the NFL is 3.5 years.

If a player has a couple of years in the league his salary has grown based on service. When camp begins and the rookie comes in, he might not be any more talented than a current player but, a team will consider the new player because of a lower salary. By not keeping a veteran player in their system he is released to fend for himself on getting the vested four years of service with another team.

I am not trying to disparage the NFL, its owners or its players. I have always been a fan and will continue to be a fan. I would have played for free just to say I played in the NFL. I want to educate any young player that has the ability to make it to the NFL to know that his playing time will end. Do not squander what you have accomplished. You never know when the career ending injury is going to occur or when you will be cut from the roster. Hang on to the bonus, salary, and any other compensation that may come your way.

You have just left college where you got by on very little. Live on the same budget—eat at the game table or what the team provides on a per diem. Put the money away and after a few years you will have a couple hundred grand in the bank and a good start to the rest of your life.

Another acquaintance that played six years of major league baseball showed me this more frugal approach to the professional athlete's path to financial stability. It is always interesting to hear the insider stuff relating to baseball including the travel, clubhouse activities, etc. He told me he was given a per diem of $125 for meals. I asked if anyone just pocketed the cash and ate a $3.99 value meal, and he responded, "Yeah, ME."

After retirement this former MLB player returned to his hometown and now operates a successful business. He was fortunate to have been drafted after earning a college degree. Baseball players face more temptation to skip college and go into the numerous rounds of draft picks that occur every year. In baseball you can be drafted right out of high school without setting foot on a college campus. However, even with a large signing bonus there is no guarantee of making it to the big leagues and your future income potential is always a gamble. Even if you eventually make the Show, there is always time spent in the low-income minor leagues.

I follow a guy from my hometown that has been successful in the major leagues. He went straight from high school to the pros and eventually made the major leagues where he has even made the All-Star team. Recently, he was negotiating a new contract and he said he needed to make as much as possible because he had a family to support and he had not attended college. Sounds like he has a good head on his shoulders and his plans have been well thought out.

We recently attended a church my wife wanted to visit. Before the service began the pastor wanted to recognize a young member that just signed a pro ball contract and was heading out that Monday to join the team. He had recently graduated from a smaller school that had made its first appearance ever in the NCAA tournament. A few days earlier he had taken a job selling insurance after the season was over. Now he was on his way to live out a dream of playing pro ball. I tracked down the team he was on and saw that he was 0 for 10 in his first at bats as a pro. I do not know how far this young man will go in the pros but I do know he has lived his dream while also acquiring a college degree that will have rewards and payoffs in his future.

Another kind of windfall scenario with rapid rises and falls is the music industry. Living in and around Music City for over 20 years I have seen a lot of overnight success. Every year a struggling artist goes from nothing to millionaire in no time. I have always heard it is harder to make it in the music industry than in pro sports. Picking up a guitar or playing the drums can happen almost anywhere, compared with playing ball which requires additional space and equipment just to practice. The competition among a thousand people playing a decent guitar would be intense compared to the handful of quarterbacks with the ability to make it to the next level.

A man can play an instrument in a band or compose music and make a living but it is extremely hard to break into the big money. When it happens you need to be prepared to tackle the success head on. A quote I have often heard around the industry is, "You're only as good as your last hit," and by "hit," I mean a song in the top ten on the charts. Anything out of the top ten is just a blip in the news.

Sometimes lightning does strike and you reach the top. I have seen it more than once and it can be a big payoff. Just remember what it took to get to that point and what has to happen to stay. I know people who have had number one hits that I am sure paid off in the millions, but to make ten million dollars in a short time, does not mean go out and buy an eight million dollar house. Before that big payoff came along you were living and maintaining on a modest income. Why not continue to live meagerly until the next number one? I am not saying don't enjoy your success, but just take it slow and see how long the quick income will last.

> **Proverbs 27:23-24** [23]Know well the condition of your flock, and pay attention to your herds, [24]for wealth is not forever; not even a crown lasts for all time.

Whether it is a gift for sport, the ability to perform musically, a head for business or any other God given talent, you should honor the Lord with what was given to you. The instruction manual of the Gospel is easy to follow. Once you get on track and follow God's word you will not only enjoy success from your talents but you will be able to help and instruct others in the ways of the Lord. You were given a talent and a chance to have success so teach and tell others what the Lord has done and what He can do for them.

I remember watching a documentary on older musicians and rock bands. They said they trusted everyone, but in truth there were a lot of people with their hands in the money. In most cases the artists were young and naive and trusted the wrong people when large amounts of cash started rolling in. They allowed someone else to control the money and throw it around with no regard for the well being of the artist who generated the income. Management takes their fee up front so if they make a poor decision it is not coming out of their pockets.

In the case above, the musician was recalling when his managers invested in Clydesdale horses. He allowed other people to use his money and they bought this team of horses as an investment. The musician said, "What do I know about Clydesdale horses?" Looking back on the failed venture the artist had to laugh about such a ridiculous purchase but I am sure the managers thought it was the best idea in the world. Besides, if it did not work out, none of their funds were risked in the investment.

Another bad idea for entertainers or athletes is to get into the restaurant business. You have made it in your industry and have had great success. Your money is starting to pile up and someone comes up with the idea for you to open a restaurant with your name on the marquee. People are telling you that having your name on the establishment is going to make it an instant success. Everyone will come because YOU are on the sign above the door.

You need to break any of the bad habits or routines that have no benefit spiritually or financially. If you hang around people that do not follow the rules or obey the law it will catch up with you in the long run and have negative effects on your life. A bad environment will not benefit you when you are striving to do the right thing and build a path for your family.

You do not need to cut off all contact with your roots but if you were once involved in things detrimental to you and your community it makes sense for you not to be around those people. If bad things are happening to the people you knew growing up you have the chance to start a new life in a new place. Do not become another statistic plaguing the neighborhood.

I recently met a friend that currently plays baseball in the major leagues. At first I thought he was just another baseball player working his way through the system. My wife had met him at our workout and training facility. I had not heard of him but after doing a little research I saw that he was a candidate for rookie of the year the prior season. After getting to know him and talking a little about baseball, I had asked why he was hanging out in Tennessee.

This player grew up in the Miami area but attended college in Tennessee. After getting to know people and enjoying Tennessee he continues his offseason training here. He stayed in Tennessee because he wanted to get away from any possible trouble around Miami. This was a smart decision by such a young person who has started reaping the payoffs of a major league ballplayer.

Again, I am not saying to abandon your old friends from your hometown but if these people are not on the same path of striving for success they will only slow your progress. There are many times when you can enjoy the success you have acquired with old friends. I met a man who played in the NFL who told me about how he would book flights for a few of his friends to hang out and enjoy the new life he had acquired from playing ball. In the same circumstances I would have done the same thing. It is fun to shower some fun on the people that you were close with in your youth. How fun it would be to have those people around when you are going through a great time in your life.

A close friend moved to the west coast and was successful with some companies he started. He would come back to our little hometown and rent a limo to shuttle a few of us around. Limos were not a common sight in our town and there was probably just one place to rent one. Cruising around town with our friends was a luxury we enjoyed. This friend worked with some big name entertainers and when these entertainers came to Nashville we would be treated to the same limo services along with a meet and greet before the show. This was always a big treat because these bands were long time staples in our cassette decks. To get to meet the rock star royalty was a pinnacle for young fans like us.

Another friend who hit it big in the entertainment industry was part of a music duo that had major success, sold millions of records and made millions of dollars in the process. We were once fairly close friends that shared the struggles of young people moving to a new town in search of success. In the summer we hung out on the local lake and took part in the social single life of the big city. Once he hit the big time he seemed to leave behind some of his friends. Maybe we were not as close as I had thought but others I knew mentioned the same feeling. He was nice enough to provide passes and meet and greets at shows and would even get passes for friends of mine that were strangers to him but it seems that fame brought about some disconnection from the old gang. Another mutual friend who had a closer relationship told me he had seen the now famous person at an event. He called out his friends' name, but got no response. To his surprise the old friend just kept moving with his entourage without even acknowledging the old friend's hello. Cutting off all contact just because of fame or success escapes me.

I have never been famous, so I do not know the pressures associated with being propelled into the public eye. I have heard of mangers, agents, attorneys, etc. trying to change the world the famous person came from and even keep them secluded from past influences. This could be a smart move if the famous person came from a place detrimental to their current state. On the other hand, if fame has caused you to distance yourself from people who were just old friends from the past you are making a mistake. Do not forget your friends and family that gave support and encouragement in the beginning.

But the main concept is to never forget where your talent and abilities came from. God provided you with all knowledge, talent and ability to get you to the pinnacle of whatever the circumstance. The first priority is to honor God for everything you are, have, or are striving to become. The term God given talent is the best description that can be given to anyone who has made it to the top level.

Matthew 7:7-8 [7]Keep asking, and it will be given to you. Keep searching and you will find. Keep knocking, and the door will be opened to you. [8]For everyone who asks receives, and the one who searches finds, and to the one who knocks, the door will be opened.

9

The Party Doesn't Last

Proverbs 23:19-21 [19]Listen, my son and be wise; keep your mind on the right course. [20]Don't associate with those who drink too much wine, or with those who gorge themselves with meat. [21]For the drunkard and the glutton will become poor, and grogginess will clothe them in rags.

I could be one of the last to lead a sermon on living right and staying off the course of indulgences of alcohol and food. I was once a heavy drinker who ate everything and anything I wanted. Both have long term, negative effects on your body. There is no difference between drinking 10 beers and eating 10 mini burgers but the consequences can vary. Consuming alcohol can cause legal trouble if you go out in public causing trouble or get behind the wheel of a vehicle.

If you are a regular at the local bar or just picking up a 12 pack for drinking at home, the best you can hope for is that you just drop a considerable amount of money on these habits. Spending a lot of money is the least of your worries. There comes a long list of problems that can be attributed to a lifestyle of continuous drinking. I am not a teetotaler, it even states in the Bible that a little wine is good for the stomach. The abuse of anything, however, especially alcohol, will not serve you well.

> **1 Timothy 5:23** Don't continue drinking water only, but use a little wine because of your stomach and your frequent illnesses.

Alcohol has caused much grief and trouble in my life. Growing up, I ran with a group of friends that frequently, if not every night, were partying and drinking. I went into my first bar at age 15. Not only did I not have a fake ID, I did not have any identification at all. Starting to drink at such a young age gave me a larger window of time to get into trouble. There is a chain of crises you are creating when you start using alcohol. From the time I was 15 until I was 18 I had all the alcohol charges twice. Two possession of alcohol by a minor, two public intoxications and, worst of all, two DUI's before graduating high school.

I had seven or eight close friends along with extended friendships with about everyone else in my town. My immediate friends were a pretty wild crowd. There was nothing mean or malicious about us but when it came to throwing a party we were some of the top hosts. There was a wide range of backgrounds in the group—one's dad was a doctor, one was an attorney, one owned a car dealership, one lived with a single mom like myself while others had more modest backgrounds. We all had the common trait of loving the girls and not being afraid to act on any situation that might come our way.

In the early '80s gas was still around 60¢ per gallon, beer was less than $10 a case (there were even cheaper options that got down as low as $4.99 for a case of returnable bottles) and mini burgers were 25¢. You did not need a whole lot of cash to hit the town at night—just enough to pitch in for gas, another few bucks for alcohol and a little left over for a late night snack if we got hungry.

Along with the booze and the girls we threw in our love for rock bands and frequent trips to concerts to support our favorite groups. We had long hair and thought we were rock stars but wearing our black concert T's was the closest we made it to the music industry. None of us knew how to sing or play any instruments so we were content to play our cassettes on our 100 plus watt car stereos. I prided myself in the ability to calculate the time of the songs that were listed on an album and I would custom record the tapes to limit the dead air at the end of each recording. It was unprofessional to have a song cut off at the end of a tape or have five minutes of blank tape left at the end of your recording. This was my great contribution to the music industry.

All joking aside, the happy go lucky rockers chasing girls and drinking away their youth were losing athletic scholarships and wasting time on the road to nowhere. One tragic event made everyone stop and slow down and take a look at what was really at stake. The loss of a young girl's life in an alcohol related traffic accident. I happened to be in the car on that unusually cold night in October. We had started the night with a stop at a liquor store to acquire a bottle of tequila. Within the hour we had finished off the bottle. We then proceeded to violate at least three laws related to underage drinking that were on the books.

After the pre-party we began our night of cruising the town to see what we could get into. We almost immediately ran into three girls from my high school. I was a junior, and as was usually the case, the youngest in the crowd. The girls had a bottle of wine they were sipping on as well. We invited them into our car for some cruising and socializing. My buddies had their eyes on two of the girls so I volunteered to drive. Knowing our alcohol consumption I headed out of town into the countryside, out of the sight of cruising police officers.

Only a few miles into the drive my friend demanded to get back behind the wheel. If I had known what was to going to happen I would have put up a fight for the keys. He immediately turned the car around and started back to town with no destination or plan. The car we were in was a boat with a large V8 that had a lot of top end speed and would go very fast, to say the least.

I remember looking over at the speedometer and seeing how fast we were going. We came to a curve before a bridge over a small river tributary. We started to slide and fish tail out of control. We made it past the bridge, then careened end over end for 376 feet, landing in a ditch upside down. The force and noise of such a traumatic event happens so fast that the shock does not arrive until a few seconds later. Panic then sets in and your only reflex is to get out and see what has happened.

Seat belts were still just an inconvenient strap that hung around inside of a car. Laws were not yet on the books to make buckling up mandatory and I knew very few people that took the time to wear their seatbelt. Needless to say, we must have been flying around inside the car. In fact, when we got to the hospital I was questioned by a state trooper about where I was sitting in the car. I must have been his last interview because after I told him I was in the backseat he stated that it was full.

I had been knocked around pretty hard but the only injury I had was a black eye. I remember being hit so hard I could not see and I thought I had lost my eye. I still remember asking everyone if my eye was there because it was not functioning just after the accident. The others' injuries were worse than mine. Everyone had major cuts or broken bones. But the most tragic part of the crash was one of the girls lost her life.

Cindy was one of the nicest, smartest, cutest girls in our high school. She was the one who stayed home during the week studying to prepare for college and moving into adulthood. I would rarely see her out, especially not on the fringes of our wild crowd. I even had a secret crush on her and once I called her at home and spoke to her. She was just a very sweet girl that every one enjoyed being around and having as a friend.

This became a nightmare, not only for the family that lost a precious loved one but also for a family that had to endure the legal issues of such a tragedy. The months that followed included a criminal trial as well as a lawsuit against the family of the driver of the car. A variety of mistakes made by a group of kids affected many people mentally, emotionally and financially. There is no dollar amount that can be put on a life but the court will arrive at an amount that will be awarded in such a case. In today's system there would certainly be jail time involved in such an accident. The only question would be how much time to give a driver under the influence of alcohol.

Back in 1981 the DUI laws were not as stringent as they are today. With the increase in alcohol related accidents there came a demand for stricter consequences for alcohol related injuries and deaths. In this case, the driver did not have to go to jail. I think the court saw a young person that made a horrible mistake and knew it would not be right to ruin another kid's life by putting him in jail. Having to live with the fact that you took another person's life is hard enough. The idea of imprisonment would not benefit anyone in a situation like this.

Another incident that occurred recently in our community illustrates the tragedy of a family involved in an alcohol related accident. I did not know the people involved but the story breaks a person's heart. It is a story of a young family just starting out with their first child. The father worked while the mother stayed home with their toddler.

This man was not a big drinker but he would have a drink now and then. It was rare for him to have a drink after work but on this instance he came home after a hard day and had a couple of glasses of wine. As he was relaxing and playing with his child while his wife was cooking dinner. She asked her husband to run to the store. The store was only two miles away and he could be back in less than ten minutes.

On the way to the store the unthinkable occurred. The man was involved in an auto accident and the driver of the other car was killed. It did not look like a serious accident but it was enough to take the life of the other driver. It was an accident but the main factor that surfaced was that the man had been drinking. Any and all other factors would be dismissed in favor of alcohol as the cause of the accident.

Present day law says liability falls directly on a driver that has been drinking. When an event like this occurs it does not matter if the driver was legally drunk. In this case the man was found guilty and had to serve jail time. This man had never been in trouble before but the law states that he must go to jail.

This is another case where not only did one family lose a loved one but another family is in ruins from a tragic mistake. This man was the head of a young, single income family that was just getting started. The result is a stay home mom that is left alone without any means of support.

Financial consequences are the least of the problems that can occur from the using alcohol. You can drop $50 to $100 dollars drinking and socializing during a night on the town but one needs to also take into account all the possibilities that can follow. Not only could you be ruined financially but you could also ruin your life or take the life of someone else.

I am not a teetotaler, anti-drink person, but I do see myself drinking less and less. With young kids involved in school activities and sports there is no time to have a drink. I might have a beer or two on occasion but any more than that and I am sure the next day I would pay a toll. Another thing I know for sure is if I drink one beer or take even one sip of an alcoholic beverage I will never get behind the wheel of a car. Knowing what can take place makes me full with fear.

This past year I coached a youth football program and one part of the coaches training process was to sign an oath at the end of the orientation. As a coach, I had to agree to not use tobacco products or drink alcohol in front of players. This was a very good insertion to the program and sets a good example for the young kids during the season. I am proud to say I have always honored this code and hope it has had some influence on at least one player during my coaching years.

During the training I also learned that outside of family and church the coach was the third contact for a player having some troubles or problems. In inner city areas the mother was the first contact and, if they attended church regularly, the pastor the second. In a lot of cases, however, the church is not present so the coach is next in line. I live and coach in a fairly affluent area so there are not a lot of single parents, although they are present in our community. In any case, I am always glad to help any young person and I try to offer the best and most accurate advice in any circumstance. If I can help anybody, especially a child, to know and walk with God's word I know I have done something good.

Proverbs 20:1 Wine is a mocker, beer is a brawler, and whoever staggers because of them is not wise.

10

A Career Restart

> **Romans 12:18-21** [18]If possible, on your part, live at peace with everyone. [19]Friends, do not avenge yourselves; instead, leave room for His wrath. For it is written: Vengeance belongs to Me; I will repay, says the Lord. [20]But if your enemy is hungry, feed him. If he is thirsty, give him something to drink. For in so doing you will be heaping fiery coals on his head. [21]Do not be conquered by evil, but conquer evil with good.

Over your working lifetime there are going to be occurrences when you have to start a new career or get back into the workforce in a different capacity. Or it just might be searching for new opportunities that in return will require you to explore options involving a career change. Remember that the same hard work can be applied to your new venture and success that occurred with your last occupation can also be obtained by the same work ethic.

My wife was out of the workforce for a few years when our children were young. She did not want to be traveling while the kids were growing up. Because she does not like to sit around she helped with the businesses I had established as much as possible. Eventually, the kids got older and she was ready to get back into her earlier career.

The insurance industry is a highly competitive business and once you get out of the game it can be difficult to catch the next wave of innovation. She began her search locally and soon found a colleague she knew from the industry. This man was starting a business related to insurance but different from her previous sales experience. My wife had been out of the market for several years and was returning to a different industry so she accepted a salary that was a fraction of what she used to earn. However, the owner did offer some revenue sharing and additional commissions based on her performance and company growth.

This looked like a great opportunity and my wife was all in. She was, for all intents and purposes, the only employee. The company did have an affiliate company that the owner used to finance his new venture. The affiliate was at a different location and provided technical and administrative assistance. This was a job where someone hands you an online directory and you start dialing for dollars. If you have never cold called, especially on the phone, you have no idea how difficult it is to make a sale. Usually, you get a quick "not interested," and then you move on to the next call. It is a hard process and if you have a thin skin you will quickly get discouraged. But my wife is a hard worker. She dug in, started getting positive results and, in return, the business started to roll in and the company began to show signs of success.

In the beginning, people would ask how she liked working for the owner. I even witnessed on separate occasions, two people at our church ask her about the job and the owner. It became a trend with people giving bad opinions and telling stories about the owner. There seemed to be a trail of questionable practices that followed the man. By all outward appearances my wife could not see any indications of bad character. He treated her well and accommodated her needs as a newly hired sales rep. He was a married man with a wife and kids and attended church. My wife is always one to share and witness and even had talked about her relationship with the Lord with the owner. Early on she told me that his only knowledge of the gospel was one Bible verse: Matthew 7:15 which talks about the wolves in sheep's clothing.

> **Matthew 7:15** Beware of false prophets who come to you in sheep's clothing but inwardly are ravaging wolves.

After some time my wife could see how this applied to her boss's life. She saw him in constant fear of people being out to get him or steal his business ideas and technology. Prospective customers and business were turned away because of his never ending paranoia of someone being "out to get him." This mindset comes from always trying to take advantage of situations to benefit yourself. When a person lies, cheats, steals or manipulates to secure his best interest he becomes aware of what can be done to him. For himself, it is acceptable behavior but when the tables are turned everybody and everyone becomes a bad risk.

This would be a sign of things to come with this man. With my wife's efforts the business started to grow rapidly and sometimes the support staff could not keep up with production. The owner even told her to slow down and not bring in any new business until they could catch up with current work. He wanted her to set up the contacts and he would take it from there. If she made contacts with higher-level executives he would jump in and act like it was his contact and take the sale. Sometimes, these contacts would ask to continue to work with my wife but she would always abide by the wishes of her employer and not buck the system.

The first year, my wife established new business relationships and generated revenue throughout the country. Now that her probationary period was over my wife and her boss agreed to renegotiate her compensation package for the second year. He did agree to raise her salary but it was still far below the industry standard and below what she had earned before. She agreed to the package because it also included insurance benefits. In addition, the carrot was still out there to earn additional commissions and revenue splits based on generated revenue.

The second year saw the company grow even bigger with new business and revenue all based on the efforts of my wife. It was then she started to see strange behavior and business practices that were not normal. The owner seemed to be paranoid of people trying to steal his ideas and increasingly turned down good opportunities. With the company growing beyond the expectations of the owner the paranoia set in again and after two years he decided that his employee and support staff needed to sign a non-compete and non-disclosure agreement.

My wife had signed non-competes and non-disclosures in the past. She wanted to be cautious and make sure she was not signing anything that could keep her from making a living in the future. She reviewed the document and was concerned about some of the language. After conveying her concerns to the owner she requested to let her attorney review it and make suggestions. The owner was annoyed and displeased with the request but my wife wanted to make sure it was fair agreement and would not hinder her future earnings.

The attorney discovered some points of concern and made some minor changes. My wife contacted the owner and requested a meeting to discuss the issues in question. The owner agreed and they set a time to iron out the agreement and strategize business for the upcoming year. In preparation, my wife downloaded the contact list she had complied over the past twenty months to pinpoint which customers and regions to target in the new year.

My wife got a call from the owner while on her way to the meeting asking to move it to the afternoon. She arrived at the office of the owner's affiliate company, and to her surprise, was followed in by a woman she knew was the human resources director. She was caught off guard but realized that this meeting was not about business development and new territories to solicit. The owner then told her this just was not going to work out because of the direction and focus of the company.

My wife did not know what to say. She had never been fired. She pleaded her case and even asked if she could at least work through Christmas. The owner said no and that now was the best time to cut ties. Then my wife's mood became angry and she said that she had never been fired in her life and was not going to start with this company. She asked to resign and for them to accept her resignation. The human resources person chimed in and said that if you quit you are not eligible for unemployment. My wife understood—her record of a spotless employment history is far more valuable than the pittance she would receive in unemployment. The owner agreed since his company would not have an unemployment claim filed against them and he could move on unaffected by the proceedings. That was the end of the 20-month stint with a new start up company owned by a man who pretended to be a Christian.

Unfortunately, the story does not end here. My wife has never been without a job in her entire working life. Even when our children were young she was always pitching in and contributing something to our household. She began a tiresome, non-stop attempt to find a job, calling everyone, expanding her social network, and sending her resume to anyone who might look at it. It was her mission to have employment secured as soon as possible. In a couple of months she started to get some interviews and the job offers followed.

My wife got a call from a company that had a similar business in the insurance industry. She interviewed and quickly was offered a position with this company. It was a much larger and established company with a staff, technology department and an actual structured organization. An offer letter, start date and orientation were then arranged in their Chicago office.

A bright Monday morning and my wife was off for a three-day meeting in Chicago to start her new job. She would meet the office staff, pick up a computer, phone, etc. Excited about the new position my wife quickly updated her professional status from executive in transition to employed with the new firm. Little did she know, her former employer was lying in wait to start a malicious, unwarranted attack. By Thursday of that first week a lawsuit against my wife was in motion. By the following Monday the papers arrived at our front door.

Here was an owner that had the best employee to promote and generate business for his new company. This employee generated hundreds of thousands of dollars in revenue and had left under what she thought were amicable conditions, was now being sued for damages with monetary relief. My wife is a person who tries hard to make people happy about themselves and nothing upsets her more than to think someone does not like her. She knew she had done nothing to harm this man or his company and she was in shock for days after the papers were delivered.

My wife's former employer hired a large firm that specialized in employment law. The attorney for this man called my wife's attorney, thinking he would get someone inexperienced who would work out an easy resolution. It almost worked because my wife's attorney advised her to settle on every complaint that came across the desk. Fortunately, we have a couple of attorney friends who were a little more knowledgeable who said there was nothing to the suit and that she should fight the case. With this advice my wife then advised her attorney that she would be getting new representation.

Meanwhile, I am fuming about the whole mess. My wife made a lot of money for this little man and he, in return, is suing her. I, of course want to be involved in the meeting with the new attorney to see if he really is capable of putting together a legitimate defense.

My wife and I sat down with the new attorney and one of the first topics of discussion are the fees involved to work on this case. He thinks the suit is without merit, but to find out for sure will require a ten thousand dollar ($10,000) retainer. Now we are five figures into a frivolous suit that has no merit or substance.

Once you turn over funds to anyone you are then at the mercy of the business, entity or service provider retained. You give them the advantage and control of the situation. In some instances, a contractor may need some materials that are necessary to complete the project, such as custom tile, but what if the tile layer needs a basic tool such as a trowel or kneepads? Why would you provide funding for items that he should already have to perform a job? Only provide what is needed to perform the initial steps of a job and pay the balance on completion of the job.

Attorneys work on a different playing field where they can ask for whatever amount sounds good at the moment. Desperate and worrisome times bring about situations where you will do anything just to get the legal problem behind you. Being at the mercy of the court, or in this case an attorney that may have some extra bills due, we forked over the amount given. We did not question the amount and, without a lot of thought, gave the attorney the money.

Everything in an attorney's world revolves around continuances, extensions, delays, etc., because in his world time is money. The client has a legal issue they are hoping to resolve and money to spend by "betting" on the chosen attorney to win the case. But the attorney is going to get paid no matter the outcome.

Now, with the attorney sitting on a chunk of our change does he need to put our case at the front of the line? Does he need to go after a speedy resolution? Does he have to call us back in a timely manner or to call us back at all? The answer would be no to all of the above. He has our cash and it comes down to his time frame to when the proceedings take place. The case, which he assures us is nonsense, will not be resolved easily or quickly.

With the first court appearance scheduled my wife is assured there is nothing to the case and it should be thrown out. If you have sat through a civil court proceeding you know that it can be long and boring but it can also be entertaining to watch the everyday citizens doing battle in the courts with the attorneys. I was there to offer support to my wife and to just stare at the plaintiff and wonder how he could put a person through such meritless suffering. It gave me some relief to see that he had two high dollar attorneys with him, each probably running about $400 an hour.

Looking back, I don't recall any cases on the docket being resolved that morning. We sat there as each case was brought to the judge and he gave judgments, postponements, continuations, etc. related to each case. They all had some legal procedure or process that just moved them on down the line for another day. And that is exactly what happened with my wife's case. Her case was the last one called and the opposing attorneys strutted through the doors as if they had just received their Harvard law degrees and accepted their first five-figure retainer check.

What I failed to notice during all the legal wrangling was that the attorneys were outside in the hallway negotiating their next move in this case. Since time is money, I am sure an agreement was reached to stall the case another 60 days and see what happens. The client's tab was open and the attorneys could always resolve this at a later date. So the attorneys rushed in and joyfully petitioned for a motion to extend the proceedings to X date.

There was some small satisfaction in watching the plaintiff's face drop and seeing him walk out like he had just lost everything. My wife's attorney had told her that the firm her former employer was using had already charged $40,000 to get the case to this point. It was amazing to see the lengths an egotistical, vindictive person will go to just to harm another individual. But as sad as he looked leaving the courtroom we were not too far off as nothing had been resolved, or even addressed, in our three hours in the courtroom.

At this point all we could do was go about our daily routine and hope the lawsuit would somehow go away. My wife continued working and she was soon approached by another company and asked if she might be interested in the work they were doing. Although related to the healthcare industry, it was a different and very new concept. With all the new legislation in the healthcare industry, this company had created a new, innovative process that would help the industry considerably.

My wife was not looking to change companies, as her current employer had treated her very well, but, as the saying goes, they made her an offer she could not refuse. Not only was the offer a good one but also she would no longer be competing in the same line of business as her previous employer. In other words, her former employer would have no reason to pursue his malicious claim that she was in a non-compete agreement. My wife negotiated with the new company until an agreement was reached. Then came the difficult task of telling her current company she was leaving.

My wife is one of those people that does not want to make anybody feel sad. She knew it was going to be a hard call to the owner and manager to deliver the news. Her main consolation was that she would no longer be pursued by the previous employer's lawsuit. She called them on a Monday to give proper notice and to wrap up any lose ends that needed to be addressed or current cases to be handed off. They were stunned and saddened by her decision but agreed that the offer was too good to pass over.

The next day, without any notice or announcement of her having left the current company or taking another position, the attorney sent over a response from the plaintiff's attorney stating that the case would be dismissed. So within five days of starting her new job my wife was presented with a lawsuit from her previous company and within five days of leaving the job it was dismissed. She says that the six months the suit was pending was one of the worst times of her life. It was hard for my wife to overcome since she has always tried to give people the benefit of kindness and love. That someone would have the hate in them to do something like her employer did was hard to accept.

I have heard the phrase "If something does not kill you it makes you stronger" and this statement proved true for us. The Lord will only allow so much to be heaped upon your back. If He is walking with you and sustaining you in troubled times it is no problem. Anything can be overcome with God's hand. By petitioning Him and asking for support and help you will overcome.

One last footnote to the whole nightmare occurred a few days after the one page dismissal document arrived by email from the attorney. In one of his few communication outreaches he calls my wife and tells her that an additional $8,100 is due for the work that was done on the case. Of course now I have rekindled the fuse that was not quit extinguished from the beginning of this whole nonsense. Here is a case that the attorney stated from day one had no merit and would be no problem to overcome, a case that was never heard before a judge and probably had a total of two hours of face-to-face meetings followed by approximately five phone calls totaling less than 30 minutes of talk time and a $10,000 retainer held by the attorney. Now additional funds are requested for services rendered. To top it all off, the first attorney that basically fielded a few phone calls, sends over a bill for over $4,000. After anger subsides you just have to laugh at both attorneys just to come down off the ledge.

> **Proverbs 28:22** A greedy man is in a hurry for wealth: he does not know that poverty will come to him.

I don't know if it is greed, desperation, or just plain dishonesty that would cause people to act like this. I know an attorney's income is based on billable hours but to just make up random bills based on personal exaggerated calculations is just wrong. With the first attorney that sent over the $4,000 bill for some minimal time involved with the case, we had just previously finished up litigation on another case where they received over $12,000 on our behalf. It was another situation where they performed very limited work and basically received that amount for using their letterhead. We did not complain but did think their fees were a little exorbitant.

I am sure I am like most people where anger will set in if you think someone is taking advantage of you or right out stealing from you. This seems to have always been my first reaction and then after years of popping off at the mouth or taking a fly off the cuff reaction I have slowed down and taken a few breaths to calm down. The scripture that best describes such situations comes in the book of James.

> **James 1:19-20** [19]My dearly loved brothers, understand this: everyone must be quick to hear, slow to speak, and slow to anger, [20]for man's anger does not accomplish God's righteousness.

11

You're (I'm) Not Preaching to the Choir

> **Matthew 7:3-5** ³Why do you look at the speck in your brother's eye but don't notice the log in your own eye? ⁴Or how can you say to your brother. "Let me take the speck out of your eye," and look, there's a log in your eye. ⁵Hypocrite! First take the log out of your eye, and then you will see clearly to take the speck out of your brother's eye.

I am writing about these things because this is what I have lived. I, and everyone else, have fallen short on the spiritual rules of finances as well as a variety of other things I have not carried out properly. Everything I have talked about so far I have done the opposite. Hopefully, my lessons and mistakes will help you and allow you to focus on real concerns instead of money.

When I first met my future wife she was working in a service capacity in the group insurance industry. She moved quickly up the ladder and over to the more lucrative sales side. Her job involved traveling all over the country, working with companies in the final stages of being sold. She was living in an apartment with a roommate and had money to spare.

During our first dates my wife told me she never balanced her checkbook. I was appalled because I kept my checking account balanced to the penny. I learned this skill in college when I might have $1.38 in my account but knew I could still write a 78¢ check for a candy bar. The challenge of balancing her checkbook that had never been balanced was a project I was willing to tackle. Using my one class in college accounting I started the process. After an hour or so I found her checking account $3500 under drawn—meaning she had $3500 extra just floating in the account. My wife knew she had enough cash to write checks, which was her only concern. She still does not balance her checking account because, as she states, "[it] does not make me any money."

After a short job stint in California I came back to Tennessee and did not have a career path planned. After a few months working for some friends with a moving business I got into the mortgage industry at the beginning of the housing boom. After a few years of working with a larger firm I knew I had the experience and expertise to start my own business. After all, mortgages are based on numbers and percentages. You help people budget for a new home and in some cases refinance their current home. I could save customers large amounts of money by restructuring their current liabilities.

My future wife was doing well and she decided to move out of her apartment and purchase a townhouse in a nicer part of town, closer to her work. Both of us were working and had a lot of disposable cash. We would take lots of trips all over the United States. Yearly ski trips to Utah, Christmas trips to New York—we hit every popular destination. We even got engaged on a ski trip to Park City, Utah.

After getting married we lived in her townhouse while

looking for a home to start a family. We looked for months but had no luck. One day, my father-in-law drove by a neighborhood we liked but was out of our price range. There was one house left that the builder was ready to sell. He agreed to a price way below the other homes in the neighborhood. Later, my father-in-law would say that the Lord led him down that street and we all agreed.

We lived in that house for four years while we had both our children. Soon after our second child was born, it was time to think about making the move to a different house. These were good times—money was flowing, we had no debt and banks were giving up the money with just a signature. In our heads we were ready for the big time. We found a lot in a neighborhood we liked and scooped it up for new construction. Our old house sold quickly so now we had a lot, some money and a set of plans for our new dream house.

I had just acquired my contractor's license and was ready to go. I had taken the test, completed the paperwork and now was a professional builder ready to construct a million dollar home. I rolled up my set of architecturally approved, three by two foot, professional plans and walked into the banker's office for my instant approval and timetable on my initial construction draw. I met with the banker, gave him my plan copies and confirmed the process of the transaction. The plans had to be reviewed and an appraisal ordered and processed to get the loan approved. This should take a few days and the banker would get back with me.

After a few days pass I start to get impatient and inquire about what is causing the delay. After some wrangling I finally got in touch with someone who informs me that this loan is not going to go through and I owe $350 for an appraisal. At this point I am fuming because of time lost and the kicker of being told I owe THEM money. How dare they not approve ME? I have no debt, sufficient income, spotless credit and money.

> **Proverbs 28:11** A rich man is wise in his own eyes, but a poor man who has discernment sees through him.

I marched into the banker's office and started screaming at anyone who might have been associated with this decision. The assistant will not give me my plans and someone calls for security. I started for the exit, but not without one last screaming demand that I had better have my plans in hand by tomorrow. At this point, my wife tried a more diplomatic approach and was able to speak with a VP of the bank. Her calm demeanor went a lot farther than mine and she negotiated that as long as I not come back to the office they would return our plans.

Not long ago, my wife mentioned to me that I was a real jerk when I had a lot of money rolling in. There are many things I am not proud of in my younger days. I was not always a pleasant person to be around. I was quick to snap at employees, colleagues or anyone else I thought was in my way. Having a little success and thinking I was the new wizard of the business world swelled my head until I believed I knew more than everyone else in the room. I thought I had it going on more than I really did. Since the bubble burst, my wife says I am a lot nicer. She does agree, though, that being nice with a little cash would not be a bad combination.

I went to two other banks and received the same turndown for a construction loan. To get approval as a contractor I was missing one major component, which was that I had never built a house. Eventually, I found a banker willing to go out on limb and approve the loan. He put in the requirement that I use an established builder as a consultant during the construction phase. I worked out a contract with the consulting builder, paid him a thousand dollars to satisfy the banker, then told the builder I will see you later. This was another arrogant, cocky move that would be a poor decision in the long run. The builder was willing, knowledgeable and competent and I could have used another set of eyes while building my house.

The house ended up taking way longer than needed to complete. Construction went way over budget and did not meet some quality standards but I believed I did not need any help. I had passed the test and I was a contractor. Soon, it became clear why bankers were cautious and needed way more than just a good credit rating for construction loans. It takes a level of expertise to build a home and, needless to say, a newly licensed contractor that has never worked in the industry has not developed that expertise.

We finally finished the house 18 months after we began the construction process. Losses, overruns and do overs probably ended up costing over $100,000. As well as other mistakes and wrong decisions that we made in the construction phase. I am not against building some projects or remodeling some small areas of a home. But I can say I will probably not be building another large project again. If you are not a professional and don't have many years of construction experience, I would not tackle such a large project. It reminds me of building a custom car or motorcycle, unless you are actually doing the wrenching and building the project yourself you are not going to come out on top with the build. The money you put into the parts and labor are lost most of the time. Something you might have dropped a lot of money into will not have the value of the money spent to complete. The same can be true about a home. Someone might have put a lot of money in and now based on market conditions will have to sell at a loss.

If you are in the market for an upgrade on a home I would check local inventory first and probably would always take this route before I started the building process. And remember to get what you can afford. Big, nice homes are cool for a while but when the yearly maintenance, utilities, cleaning, and basic upkeep never stops they sometimes become more than you expected. The small, cozy home with just the basics sounds better and better each day.

Based on certain formulas, my wife and I had a multi-million dollar net worth, but elaborately prepared accounting sheets and actual cash in the bank are two very different ways to asses your wealth. Adding up all our assets and subtracting our liabilities showed us with a net worth of about $2.4 million. This number looks good to the banker who wants you to take the unsecured credit line for a $100,000, which we did. The banker also noticed we had a lot of equity in our house and set us up with another $100,000 line of credit. For our new business, the banker recommended an unsecured $50,000 credit line. They all sounded good, Mr. Banker and we took it all.

It has been a long hard road to dig out of the debt we accumulated when I was in business for myself and acquiring too much. Slowly, my wife and I have moved out from under the pile of debt but there is still a long way to go to be completely recovered. I look back on the wealthy days when there seemed to be no worries about money and no end to comfortable living. Any good financial advisor or money manager should tell you it does not last. At some point, the star athlete with a thousand yard season, the music artist with a number one hit or the sales executive leading his company will see it all come to a screeching halt. What is important is how well you have planned for that day so you can maintain your lifestyle when it happens.

Jeremiah 9:23-24 [23]This is what the Lord says: The wise must not boast in his wisdom; the mighty must not boast in his might; the rich must not boast in his riches. [24]But the one who boasts should boast in this, that he understands and knows Me—that I am the Lord, showing faithful love, justice, and righteousness on the earth, for I delight in these things.

12

No Debt

Romans 13:8 Do not owe anyone anything, except to love one another, for the one who loves another has fulfilled the law.

One step to being financially secure is to not spend what you cannot afford. When you start a trend of over extending you are headed for trouble. I am all about fun, vacations, or any other recreation that may cost some money. I enjoy motorcycles, water sports, snow skiing, sporting events and concerts, among other things. However, if you are charging your plane tickets or putting your hotel room on a credit card you are not going to be having fun once the bills come.

The same rule applies to vehicles. If you are currently driving a car payment you cannot afford your car. I have heard the argument that "I can afford this payment and I like getting a new car but I just don't have the $30,000 in hand to pay for it." So, you finance the vehicle for 60 months and hope that after that time you will have a paid off vehicle in good shape. After five years of making all the payments at five percent interest you come out paying a total of $4000 above the original price and then you are left with a five year old vehicle that no longer has a fourth of its original value.

Other people make the argument that they have the zero percent financing deal on their vehicle. What these people don't realize is they are paying full sticker and, in some cases, the price is inflated to make up for any lost financing charges. Also, it is a guaranteed that there will be no price negotiating on any zero percent financing programs.

Still, others may try to sell you on the lease program being offered by the dealer. This is the worst possible form of driving a vehicle. You would do just as well to go to the airport, negotiate a weekly or monthly rate, and drive off in a rental car. That way you get to drive a new car every week or month at about the same price. A lease is basically the same thing as renting a car for an extended time and then giving it back at the end of the period. Moreover, if you go over the mileage allotment there will be a substantial penalty.

By no means am I saying you should drive an old piece of junk. I am saying you should pay for what you have and not drive something that is declining in value while you are still making payments. When people ask me, "What is your favorite car?" I always respond, "A paid off car." I love cars now but it is not in the budget to buy a new car and our family continues to drive the same vehicles we have had for a while.

If you take care of your car it will take care of you. My wife and I currently have three vehicles and rotate which vehicle we drive based on gas in the tank and the distance we are driving that day. The newest vehicle is driven the least because it gets very poor gas mileage. However if it is an occasion when we would rather drive a better looking vehicle it is the top choice. Our other two vehicles were both purchased before our children were born. Both are still in good condition and have been exceptional vehicles that I would purchase again. We are still driving these vehicles while our children our young. Personally, I am content with any vehicle with heat/air, radio and seats clean enough that I do not stick to them.

A friend of ours recently asked my opinion on finances. This man is a young pastor with five children and his income was not substantial enough while his wife was still at home with the kids. A friend of his who was a stockbroker had discussed some investment opportunities with the pastor but it did not sound like a good route. I agreed with him and would not gamble my money in the volatile market we are experiencing today. I told him if I were going to throw any money into the investment arena real estate would probably be the safest bet, but even today there are no guarantees. The best thing to do now is just save what you can.

In truth though, this young father of five is probably in one of the best positions I have seen in a long time. He and his father built his home and he has no debt on the residence. It is a very nice house in a great location. There are some unfinished areas in the basement and since it is owned free and clear he can finish the work anytime.

Recently, this pastor had gone to his bank and one of the loan officers was hard selling him on a HELOC (Home Equity Line of Credit). Having never had any debt outside of a small car loan it made sense that the banker would be chomping at the bit to give this man anything he wanted. When I worked in the mortgage industry I would offer HELOCs to people everyday. Usually people would already have a first mortgage and whatever equity they had above the balance of the first mortgage would be the amount of the credit line, sometimes up to 100% of the value of the home. In the case of my friend with no first mortgage, the bank would be loaning as a first mortgage only.

My advice to the pastor was to not take the loan they offered. Banks make it sound easy and inviting but once you take the first draw off the line of credit it becomes a loan and a loan means debt. One of my main points in this book is NO DEBT. My friend is rare and lucky to be under forty years of age with a free and clear house. If you can reach the goal of living without a mortgage you are way ahead of the masses and on your way to financial security and stability.

A million dollar home is fine and living in the lap of luxury seems to be a comfortable way to spend your life. There is one rule to follow though and it is if you are in a million dollar home you better have the money in the bank that you owe on the home. An even better position would be to own the home free and clear. When you own an expensive and high end property the outlay of cash does not stop with a mere mortgage. There are many monetary variables attached to such a property.

You are going to incur bills and payments of some kind for the rest of your life. Such items as utilities, insurance premiums, food, clothing and taxes are going to come due regularly. A lot of times you can estimate and come close to what you need to budget for such expenditures but there can be unseen surprises that cause these payments to spike and go above what you have budgeted. One thing that has become evident is that the cost of all the items listed above never goes down. Over time the cost of these necessities has only risen and in some cases it goes beyond what some households can afford.

My dad was fortunate enough to retire with a full benefits package. Every year he receives a packet that describes new coverage plans that are available to retirees. They make it sound like it is the new best coverage available but in reality it is not anything near what was given to him at retirement years ago. Big companies are just trying to get employees to enroll in a program that will have the employee or in this case the retiree to come out of pocket with more of their own money to cover any medical procedures. Year after year he just tears up the new offers he receives and continues with the better coverage that was offered from the beginning.

In years past if you had some form of insurance it would more than likely pay for just about 100% of what was required. But in today's ever changing economy it seems that premiums become higher and higher and coverages have decreased as far as what it being paid out on any claims. A good example took place when are children were born. Our first child was born and we were covered by my wife's insurance policy she carried through her employer. She worked for a very large organization that was an insurance company. We did not pay out of pocket one dime with the delivery of our first born.

Then almost two years to the day our second child was born. My wife still worked for the same company and had what we thought was the same insurance coverage. As it turned out there must have been changes to the policy because we ended up paying out of pocket about $2000 on the delivery of our second baby. In a matter of two years the internal changes within the company must have scaled back on policy provisions and in return charges were placed upon the employee.

My dad has even stated how his excellent insurance coverage, which still pays close to 100% of any medical procedures, now has seen additional bills associated with the coverage. Now he says when he goes into the doctor he will get a bill associated with the visit. It is never much but it is still something he now receives that was never the case in prior years.

Healthcare will be another trend we will have to account for as we carry on with life. Another bill or payment that we will not really know what the amount may be or when it will be part of a monthly outlay. It falls into that category of expenditures that will be part of your life whether you have additional debt or not. The main concept I am trying to deliver is that with all of our unforeseen bills, payments and additional debt does not need to be listed in your budget. It is hard and costly enough to just exist, let alone taking on additional amounts of debt.

Psalm 37:23-26 ²³A man's steps are established by the Lord, and he takes pleasure in his way. ²⁴Though he falls, he will not be overwhelmed, because the Lord holds his hand. ²⁵I have been young and now I am old, yet I have not seen the righteous abandoned or his children begging bread. ²⁶He is always generous, always lending, and his children are a blessing.

13

Hope is in the Lord

> **Philippians 4:19** And my God will supply all your needs according to His riches in glory in Christ Jesus.

A lot of our financial situation can be attributed to the local economy or government. Over the past few presidential elections in the United States we have seen a close split among the voting public. There are two parties that offer differing social and fiscal perspectives. The conservative view offers less government, letting people and businesses run their own course to accomplish their goals. The liberal view offers bigger government with more entitlements and more taxes to cover the costs.

Does either party have all the right answers to satisfy the election interests of all the people? Of course not. There will always be issues unpopular with people who have different agendas. No party will be able to satisfy everyone everywhere but we can hope for a person in charge who can make fair decisions that will benefit the populous as a whole. Many issues have common sense solutions but with the one-sidedness of the two major parties you end up with officials that just throw values and right-minded decisions out the window.

While writing this book, the debate raged about the raising of the debt ceiling for our government. This issue could be the most idiotic conversation that has occurred in our nations history. The first question is "has there ever been an attempt to lower our debt ceiling?" The second question is "how can increasing our debt limit and borrower capacity benefit anyone?"

Almost every adult in America has had a credit card at some time during his or her life. If you have never had a credit card I applaud you for your control of your finances. In college, the bank and credit companies would set up a kiosk and with just a signature you could walk away with a free hat and a credit card with a $500 limit. It seemed like these signups always occurred just before spring break. The blessed recipient would get a new wardrobe ensemble, buy a round of drinks at the pub and a late night meal and within 48 hours the card was maxed out. At the time we thought it was funny but in reality you had a kid with no job, with an over the limit credit card, paying fees and interest on $500. With a minimum payment of $39 it would take years to pay off a $500 shopping spree.

I am sure at sometime you have maxed out a credit card. This is not fun because the penalties and interest kick in and you are stuck paying a bill that never goes away. Recent legislation has helped to limit the exorbitant interest banks could make off these indebted individuals but, in reality, the credit card holder is responsible for allowing his debt to get out of control. When a credit card is at its borrowing limit why would an institution raise the limit on the card? I pose the same question to our government. Congress has consistently raised the debt ceiling over the years and I want to know if is there ever going to be a plan to pay it down?

The concept of a credit card is ridiculous. As a society we have an "I want it now. I can't afford it but I am getting it anyway" philosophy. I grew up with this philosophy and it has taken a few years to overcome it. In better economic times, my wife and

I had a successful business, great incomes, positive cash flow and adequate savings. Once we were on the radar of financial institutions we became a target for additional services in the form of unsecured loans, credit extensions, etc. I fell for these sales pitches and ended up as deep as one can get with credit.

At our bank, the cashier would offer a $25,000 credit card every day. After a few tries the cashier succeeded in signing me up. Then the branch manager offered me a $100,000 unsecured line of credit and another $100,000 credit line on my business. When it was all said and done we had over $300,000 worth of unsecured credit granted by just a signature. At one point we had the full $300,000 out on credit. Those days of bankers throwing out unsecured debt is long over and, in today's economy, there is no need to borrow money outside of purchasing a house.

I once worked in the small consumer finance business. These are the local lenders who offer small loans, from $1000 to $3000, secured with personal property. Items such has jewelry, furniture, electronics, etc. were put up as collateral and if you did not pay an employee would go to the house of the borrower to get payment or take possession of the collateral.

Working there, I had two jobs to perform and they started on the first day of the month. The first job was to call and solicit all the up to date customers to offer them more money and keep them on the books for life. The second job was to call and collect from all the people who were continuously late. It was a challenge every month to get them into the office. I never understood the mathematical structure of these loans but I knew that if you borrowed $1000 and made your scheduled payments for nine months, you would still have a balance due of around $1080. As a result, the customer would pay on loans for long periods of time but the balance would hardly move at all.

A similar lending practice has developed in the form of check cashing stores. These are just small advances at high interest rates that are not favorable to the consumer. Anything that has high rates of interest tied to the transaction should be avoided.

---

2 Thessalonians 3:6-13 ⁶Now we command you, brothers. In the name of our Lord Jesus Christ, to keep away from every brother who walks irresponsibly and not according to the tradition received from us. ⁷For you yourselves know how you must imitate us, we were not irresponsible among you; ⁸we did not eat anyone's bread free of charge; instead, we labored and toiled, working night and day, so that we would not be a burden to any of you. ⁹It is not that we don't have the right to support, but we did it to make ourselves an example to you so that you would imitate us. ¹⁰In fact, when we were with you, this is what we commanded you: "If anyone isn't willing to work, he should not eat." ¹¹For we hear that there are some among you who walk irresponsibly, not working at all, but interfering with the work of others. ¹²Now we command and exhort such people, by the Lord Jesus Christ, that quietly working, they may eat their own bread. ¹³Brothers, do not grow weary in doing good.

I recently saw a report on how the state of Texas was doing well despite the grim unemployment rate nationally. As a state governed by different values than other parts of the country it has added tens of thousands of jobs to its economy. The authors of the report criticized the employment numbers by pointing out Texas has only added low paying or minimum wage jobs. I wanted to scream back at the television, "Hey they are JOBS."

Over the years we have created an entitlement society where

people have the mindset that they "deserve" or are owed something. I see it in advertising campaigns where they say, "Get the car," or "Get the credit you deserve." Many people, however, do not want to work at the wage that is available and would rather sit back and collect a check from programs created by our government. Some charitable programs are valid and some recipients are qualified and should be helped. On the other hand, however, there are also able-bodied people who take advantage of these benefits and abuse the system.

Some people have been in these programs for generations and it has become a way of life. These people are unable to navigate a way out of this cycle. A low paying or minimum wage opportunity may offer more income but they prefer to receive their monetary support from the government. I understand that there are genuine cases for some forms of assistance but there are also drug users, criminals and other troublemakers receiving payments. I recently saw an online campaign to pass a law requiring all recipients of public assistance to submit to a drug test. If such a law were implemented there would be an uproar about civil rights being violated while trying to prevent our tax dollars being used for illegal activities. Despite all the criticism and up roar of doing drug testing for welfare participants some states have implemented the practice. Hopefully there will be some positive results from this process.

Dependence on government programs has been passed down from generation to generation and it is hard to break the cycle. I once heard that there should be only one thing offered by our government: freedom. Freedom to pursue and achieve whatever goals you set for yourself. Today, it seems a lot of people are in pursuit of whatever they can get for free.

Romans 13:1-7 [1]Everyone must submit to the governing authorities, for there is no authority except from God, and those that exist are instituted by God. ²So then, the one who resists the authority is opposing God's command, and those who oppose it will bring judgment on themselves. ³For rulers are not a terror to good conduct, but to bad. Do you want to be unafraid of the authority? Do good and you will have its approval. ⁴For government is God's servant to you for good. But if you do wrong, be afraid, because is does not carry the sword for no reason. For government is God's servant, an avenger that brings wrath on the one who does wrong. ⁵Therefore, you must submit, not only because of wrath, but also because of your conscience. ⁶And for this reason you pay taxes, since the authorities are God's public servants, continually attending to these tasks. ⁷Pay your obligations to everyone: taxes to those you owe taxes, tolls to those you owe tolls, respect to those you owe respect, and honor to those you owe honor.

Recently, a big debate that has taken place in our country has been about healthcare. A plan was implemented via government wrangling and what seemed to be a secret vote. Representatives voted for the legislation and then admitted they had not even read the bill. Of course, it was a topic that was completely split among party lines. It amazes me that an issue that needs to be addressed to benefit the whole country ends up being split along party lines. It seems that none of our representatives have the best interest of the public in mind but only what will pacify their constituents long enough to be re-elected for another term.

The healthcare issue is complex at every level and everyone has opinions about how to resolve it. There are good points on both sides of the aisle that could be implemented to solve the problems in the healthcare industry. I know for certain that we do not need government involvement in an industry that has always operated privately. The government will require revenue to sustain its program that can only be generated by additional national debt or tax increases.

The new law that went into effect was recently sent to the Supreme Court to validate its legality. This was an important step to see if the law was constitutionally sound and should be carried out for the people of the United States of America, one nation under God. The Supreme Court makes the final ruling on the laws of the land and is made up of nine justices, appointed by a president for life. Of course, the president appointing a Supreme Court justice makes sure the appointee falls in line with the political party they represent. After all, you build support with the players from your team.

Concerning the healthcare decision that took place recently, the court was comprised of four justices on the president's team and the other five justices on the team trying to get the law thrown out as unconstitutional. The Supreme Court is the ultimate all-star team—nine people at the top of their field, working their way up to the pinnacle of their profession. Being at the top of their game, Supreme Court justices are expected to perform with professionalism and rule on cases based on the facts. As if scripted, however, eight of the justices based their decision purely on party affiliation. The one remaining justice was also expected to invalidate the law by giving the ruling that his party wanted.

Then, to the amazement of the country and both political parties, the ninth justice, Chief Justice John Roberts, actually did his job interpreting the law and delivering a decision based on his legal opinion. Instead of making his decision based on what his party wanted him to do he used his knowledge of the law to make his decision. One important insight into his decision was that he way the legislation as a tax. When the law was pushed through congress it was never labeled a tax and since a majority of lawmakers did not read the law most did not know it was a tax either. Now there is a law on the books that was deceptively approved and we have yet to see what impact it will have on our country in the future.

Our country was formed as a country under God. Our forefathers established this country with God above everything and intended Him to be the main focus of the pursuit of life, liberty and happiness. Our currency reads "In God We Trust" and our Pledge of Allegiance says we are "One Nation Under God." Today, many people are trying to extract God from our daily activities whenever they can. Eliminating prayer groups in schools, not allowing pre-game prayers at sporting events and other public recognition of God have been targets of attacks from legal organizations opposed to these basic ideals of our nation.

Governments will always have authority over us and we may not agree with their policies and practices but Romans 13 states we must submit to governing authorities for there is only one true authority and that is God. He has established and instituted the governing bodies that exist. We may not understand His purposes, but the government has been put there for a reason and, in the long run, God's plan will endure.

Currently, the Ten Commandments are displayed in our Supreme Court's Hall of Justice. I just hope the Commandments will stay as a reminder of how and why our country was established. Learning about the American Revolution, I believe it was a miracle or an act of God that we became a nation. The odds were stacked against the revolutionaries as they clashed with a powerhouse like Great Britain, but a bunch of ragtag colonists and freedom seekers overcame insurmountable odds to create a new nation. Hopefully, we will see an end to the nonsensical legal wrangling to have the Ten Commandments removed from schools and courthouses throughout the United States. It amazes me how people have the time and hatefulness to pursue an agenda that benefits no one when there are so many other important things we need to accomplish as a nation.

> **John 15:6-8** ⁶If anyone does not remain in Me, he is thrown aside like a branch and he withers. They gather them, throw them into the fire, and they are burned. ⁷If you remain in Me and My words remain in you, ask whatever you want and it will be done for you. ⁸My Father is glorified by this: that you produce much fruit and prove to be My disciples.

14

Give to the Lord What is His to Begin With

Ecclesiastes 5:10-12 ¹⁰The one who loves money is never satisfied with money, and whoever loves wealth is never satisfied with income. This too is futile. ¹¹When good things increase, the ones who consume them multiply; what, then, is the profit to the owner, except to gaze at them with his eyes? ¹²The sleep of the worker is sweet, whether he eats little or much; but the abundance of the rich permits him no sleep.

I am a believer that if you work in a way that does not honor the Lord you work in futility. Even though you might see some success from your labor it will not last. Keep the focus on the most important thing, the One who gave you the ability and knowledge to succeed and is in charge of all—your Lord and Savior. If you are trying to accumulate as much as possible and store up money for your own desires what good is that going to achieve? Nothing, except to live in and be caught up in our earthly world that has no eternal value.

> **Proverbs 3:9-10** ⁹Honor the Lord with your possessions and with the first produce of your entire harvest; ¹⁰then your barns will be completely filled and your vats will overflow with new wine.

Monetarily, the Lord asks very little of you. He needs nothing, so your money and possessions are worthless to him. What does the Lord require of the money, gold or other valuable goods you may have? He only asks that you commit to Him and show your honor to the one that made you. He protects you and gives you the promise of never-ending life if only you believe in and worship Him. I wonder what people would pay if this message were put into a marketed, advertised campaign promotion. An advertisement on the front page of a paper or magazine, or a pop-up ad running across your computer stating, "You can have it all! How much are you be willing to give?" Our Lord makes it easy if only we listen and walk in His word. Money driven, possession crazed individuals would offer millions to actually "Have it all."

> **Luke 12:15-21** ¹⁵He then told them, "Watch out and be on guard against all greed because one's life is not in the abundance of his possessions." ¹⁶Then He told them a parable: "A rich man's land was very productive." ¹⁷He thought to himself, "What should I do, since I don't have anywhere to store my crops?" ¹⁸"I will do this," he said. "I'll tear down my barns and build bigger ones and store all my grain and my goods there." ¹⁹Then I'll say to myself, "You have many goods stored up for many years. Take it easy; eat, drink and enjoy yourself."

> [20]But God said to him, "You fool! This very night your life is demanded of you. And the things you have prepared—whose will they be?" [21]"That's how it is with the one who stores up treasure for himself and is not rich toward God"

As far as our earthly commitment to the Lord, He asks only a ten percent tithe of our income and receivables. He suggests greater offerings in the form talents, time or other intangible offerings we can provide. To ignore such a small request by the Lord is incomprehensible considering what Jesus gave up for us. He gave His life so that we would have everlasting life. He took the sins of the world onto His shoulders for us.

> **John 3:16** For God loved the world in this way: He gave His One and only Son, so that everyone who believes in Him will not perish but have eternal life.

There are many people out there who think of themselves as indestructible because of their accomplishments, money and power, but what is money and power to the One who created it all? What can you buy in God's kingdom with all your earthly riches and influences? You might be able to sit in the front row of an event or enjoy first class seats around the world, but if you have not given your life to the Lord you are a mere vapor of smoke that will be gone when your time is up. I remember a quote from the movie *Wall Street* that stated, "How many yachts can you water ski behind?" This shows a skewed perception of money: whatever you have is not enough. I am not disparaging the rich. I strive to have enough wealth to enjoy fun activities and I certainly would not mind skiing behind a yacht. The first thing I try to teach our children, though, is to be rich toward God before all other things. He has a hand in all our actions so fun and enjoyment are no exception to what He grants us.

---

2 Corinthians 9:6-9 [6]Remember this: the person who sows sparingly will also reap sparingly, and the person who sows generously will also reap generously. [7]Each person should do as he has decided in his heart—not out of regret or out of necessity, for God loves a cheerful giver. [8]And God is able to make every grace overflow to you, so that in every way, always having everything you need, you may excel in every good work. [9]As is written: He has scattered; He has given to the poor; His righteousness endures forever.

A recent sermon by my pastor explained how you should give as to honor the Gospel. I have been a tither to the penny for all of my years attending church as a married member. It is something my wife and I agree to do and it has become our practice to give our tithes and offerings each week. However, the habit of cutting a check week after week does not satisfy the act of the tithe. I perceive myself as the happy giver; turning over my funds to the church without complaint or grumble, but just doing it out of habit is not what God is looking for. He wants you to honor his Word with your tithe and to use your offering to reflect upon the Gospel.

What good am I doing by turning over my tithe and then not living in the word of the Lord? I have to work daily on living in the ways that makes God happy instead of living in what makes me happy. I can cut all the checks and give my last dime but unless I have turned over my heart to the word my money, talent and time are wasted. To me it is right to give what is outlined in the Bible, but it takes time and effort to get other things right that the Lord wants us to do. Loving your neighbor, loving your wife as the Lord loved the church, and living with a patient heart are just a few of things I have to get right in my daily living.

Matthew 23:23 Woe to you, scribes and Pharisees, hypocrites! You pay a tenth of mint, dill, and cumin, yet you have neglected the more important matters of the law-justice, mercy and faith. These things should have been done without neglecting the others.

My wife and I had been members of the same church for 14 years. We attended for four years before becoming members. At the time we joined the church it was growing and was located in a smaller facility. Our new members class was held in a small bakery/deli in the downtown area of our city. During the classes, the church was building a new facility and the teaching pastor requested a debt elimination campaign to help with the added expenses of construction of the new facility. We were proud to be among the first new members of the brand new church campus.

A few years ago, I was nominated to be a Deacon in the church. I humbly accepted and proceeded through the four-month orientation and study prep for the position. It was a good experience to walk with the leaders and learn more about the duties and processes involved with a large congregation. At the same time, I learned how to minister and walk with members through difficult times. As Deacons, you work in conjunction with the elders of our church to address issues and set goals and guidelines within the church. You are also part of a larger governing body that has a book of order to follow as a member of the larger affiliation.

After being installed as a Deacon you become involved in decision-making within the church. There are many procedural rules that come from the church order. One of the big topics that took up most of my first year as a Deacon was a budget crisis. Being new to the process and not really understanding all that was going on I mostly observed the proceedings. It seemed like there were a lot of committee and closed-door sessions that did not reveal many details. Looking back, I should have been more involved with asking questions on exactly what was going on but I trusted the elders had everything under control.

I still don't know exactly what took place, but I recall the actions taken during this budget crisis. The church was coming up short on expenses and the committees started to look at salaries as an area that could be trimmed. Initially, the church leadership decided that instead of making salary cuts they would just eliminate one of the pastors. They even went as far as to send out an announcement that this pastor's job was going to be eliminated.

The congregation was in shock for a few days, but then people started speaking up questioning this decision. The church leadership soon reversed their decision and all the pastors were retained on staff with pay cuts to resolve the budgets deficits. One pastor did resign. Money was never brought up as a reason but one would have to assume that his family of six would need every additional dollars to get through today's economy.

After working with the church leaders for a few years I know more about church budgets and the processes involved in church operations. The one thing I know about budgeting is that there are two variables that affect the bottom line: either too much is going out or not enough is coming in. Whatever the salaries of our pastors, they are not the problem at this church. This church's issue would be not enough coming in. I like what one of the pastors said right before taking up the offering one Sunday, "We have all the money we need for this church, it is just there in your wallets and purses."

One of our lead pastors said we are a $100,000,000 church. Based on membership numbers and the economic make up of our community the congregation should consist of an aggregate income of around $100 million. We then should have tithes and offerings at least in the 10 million dollar range. This figure states gross income numbers, actual net income would be more in the range of $60 to $70 million. I have had many conversations about whether you should tithe off your gross or net income. To me, gross pay is a fantasy number and what you take home is your income. If you receive a refund at the end of the year you can then tithe from that and this should cover any shortfall of your 10% tithe. Taxes have to be paid and this will always be true.

Matthew 22:17-21 [17]Tell us, therefore, what You think. Is ti lawful to pay taxes to Caesar or not? [18]But perceiving their malice, Jesus said. "Why are you testing Me, hypocrites? [19]Show Me the coin used for the tax." So they brought Him a denarius. "Whose image and inscription is this?" He asked them. [21]Caesar's they said to them, "Therefore give back to Caesar the things that are Caesar's, and to God the things that are God's.

This church has never really addressed the issue of tithing and I brought this up a few times at meetings. There have been conversations and suggestions that they should try to get the individual giving up from three to four percent to be able to run operations within budget. I have never seen three percent or four percent anywhere in the Bible, but if you present these numbers to the congregation, I suspect they will become the target for the members to follow.

I am sure there are many people in this church who live better Christian lives than I and who follow His word more diligently than I, but tithes and offerings are the easiest practice to put in place as a Christian. God created you and gave you everything you have. How hard is it to give back 10% to carry on His word and ministry. I am no holier, or more righteous because I give to the Lord what is his to begin with, but his word clearly states the practice of tithing is not optional.

> **Malachi 3:8-10** [8]"Will a man rob God? Yet you are robbing Me!" You ask: "How do we rob You?" "By not making the payments of 10 percent and the contributions. [9]You are suffering under a curse, yet you-the whole nation-are still robbing Me. [10]Bring the full 10 percent into the storehouse so that there may be food in My house. Test Me in this way", says the Lord of Hosts. See if I will not open the floodgates of heaven and pour out a blessing for you without measure.

The Deacons in church are in charge of a benevolence fund that helps members of our church with monetary emergencies. A lot of distribution is for counseling. Other times it is used to help with rent, utilities or other daily living needs. One of our Deacons holds the book and distributes the funds when needed. I never held the book and really don't know the exact procedure for disbursing funds. I would like to implement a counseling program for whoever may be in monetary distress.

Instead of just giving them a fish, start teaching them how to fish. Also I want to ask if they were tithing properly as directed in the Bible.

I believe if you follow the word of God in tithing you will never be in need. However, regular tithing does not guarantee you will never have financial difficulties in your life. We will all experience a monetary shortfall at some point in life but money is chaff, stubble and hay in the Lord's eyes. Money has no value or use in His heavenly kingdom but it is needed to support His church and help others along the way.

We ended up changing churches with one of the main reasons being their lack of delivering the Word about tithing. Until you address the issue of giving and offering within the church body I believe you will struggle financially as a congregation. The current church we attend is a large church about the same size as our previous one. They recently just announced the yearly budget numbers and the current year was over one million in the black.

> **Acts 20:33-35** ^{33}I have not coveted anyone's silver or gold or clothing. ^{34}You yourselves know that these hands have provided for my needs, and for those who were with me. ^{35}In every way I've shown you that by laboring like this, it is necessary to help the weak and to keep in mind the words of the Lord Jesus, for He said, "It is more blessed to give than to receive."

15

Gospel vs. Religion: Fear Not

2 Timothy 3:1-5 ¹But know this: difficult times will come in the last days. ²For people will be lovers of self, lovers of money, boastful, proud, blasphemers, disobedient to parents, ungrateful, unholy, ³unloving, irreconcilable, slanderers, without self-control, brutal, without love for what is good, ⁴traitors, reckless, conceited, lovers of pleasure rather than lovers of God, ⁵holding to the form of religion but denying its power. Avoid these people.

During a recent sermon the pastor made the statement "He could not stand religion." He explained how a religion and set of guidelines a congregation might be following means nothing. You need to be following the Gospel, which is the written word in the Bible. I think today some churches get too involved in doctrines, procedures, and other related items that are not in the Bible so they lose touch with what is of most importance. You will never go wrong referring to the Bible for any situation.

Reading 2 Timothy 3, I know I have been guilty of all of

these. I have enjoyed the fruits of money and the fast and fleeting pleasures it has brought. I have been boastful and proud of accomplishments I have made either in work, sports or school. I could not count the times I was disobedient to my parents or ungrateful to the point of being a spoiled brat.

I have been unloving towards people to the point of losing self-control and wanting to punch someone in the mouth. This anger escalates into slanderous and coarse talk towards people I believe have wronged me or my family. Then I reach the point where I am just out to please myself with no regard for the real solution of loving God. If you put your focus and life in the hands of God, He will get you through all difficulties. By putting Him first the path will become clearer and you will begin to focus on what is really important.

You will be hard pressed to find someone that is not guilty of sin on a daily basis. We were all born into sin and to completely remove it from our daily existence is impossible. We can get on better tracks and take different paths to live a more spiritual life but we all fall way short of a sinless life. Some "religious" people rely on "religion" to solve all their problems but simply practicing "religion" is not a true way of life. You need to follow the gospel, which is the word of God.

I recall attending a wedding at a one of these so-called churches. Prior to the wedding there was a rehearsal dinner where the lady minister got up to provide the invocation for the night. It was the most bizarre religious act I had ever witnessed. She proceeded to thank the dirt and the vegetables, the trucks that delivered the vegetables, the silverware we were eating with and on and on. At no point did she mention God and anything close to asking for a blessing from God. This experience made me aware of people or organizations disguised as religious groups that have no role in delivering the gospel. There are many false prophets among us in the world who operate by deceptive means or just don't know the truth about the gospel.

My wife and I volunteered at a Christian based youth camp a few years ago. My wife had been involved with many youth camps as a camper and counselor, working with youths who had little or no exposure to the true word of God. I had never been to a church camp in my life and did not know what to expect or what kind of role I could play. The actual counselors were young adults who had once been campers or were youth ministers in their local churches. My wife and I volunteered as activity instructors in art and football, respectively.

It was an amazing experience over the week at the camp. Kids came from a wide range of ethnic, socio-economic and cultural backgrounds. We came to the camp as volunteers to try to give these kids hope, encouragement and some groundwork for receiving the word of the Lord and the good He has in store for them. What I did not realize was what I would learn from my experiences with these kids. At certain times during the day the kids would gather and sing songs from popular Christian bands in a praise and worship setting. This was a fun time and seemed to be loved by the campers. I would relax and sit against the wall, watching and enjoying the happiness that was vibrating throughout the room.

I became emotional seeing all these wonderful kids, who may have had nothing materially, praising the word of the Lord in song. There were refugees from the Sudan, inner city kids, boys from a home for troubled youths, and teenage girls that had no home at all in the crowd. An African American kid sat down beside me and put his arm around me and just sat there without saying a word. Here I was, someone that had it all in terms of a family, nice home, cars and material things. Then I see a poor little boy being attentive to me and comforting me as if he knew I needed help. What an eye opener—to put things into perspective and open our hearts to see that there is a bigger picture where the ultimate goal is to follow the word of God.

During the week at camp some kids started questioning me

about church, the Word and all the messages that come with the camp experience. They were confused about the whole process. This was my first time ever to minister to young people and I did not have much experience relaying a gospel message. God put the right words into my heart and mouth and I shared my thoughts. I recommended that they read the Bible to lay the groundwork for understanding all the messages they would hear, and if they were hearing messages that were not consistent to the Gospel they should get up and run.

> **Revelation 22:18-19** [18]I testify to everyone who hears the prophetic words of this book: If anyone adds to them, God will add to him the plagues that are written in this book. [19]And if anyone takes away from the words of this prophetic book, God will take away his share of the tree of life and the holy city, written in this book.

Be careful where you go to receive your message. There are many churches or groups out there distorting and teaching false religions and if you are not careful the results could be terrible. As I told the young kids at camp, if you are not sure about what you are hearing go to the Bible. This will not only give you the truth but will help guard you against false prophecy. The Bible is the guidebook for life and a reference to living your life in a way that honors God and no one else.

> **2 Timothy 1:7** For God has not given us a spirit of fearfulness, but one of power, love, and sound judgment.

The short but effective scripture of 2 Timothy 1:7 is a powerful message that everyone should heed. If you carry around a spirit of fear it will be hard to get anything accomplished. Throughout your life you will experience fear and doubt and it will be on top of you like a weight. Let these situations be the time to call on God for direction and understanding. Fear can come on you at many stages of life. Our kids worried about the dark or what lurked beyond their comfort area by our side. I remember them creeping down the hall and then I yelled out, trying to scare them and make them run. This resulted in a quick reprimand from my wife who wondered why I wanted to scare my children and let them develop a spirit of fear. She quickly produced the scripture above and I took it to heart.

I think what God is describing in the scripture is to not fear living everyday. For kids, the dark or being away from their parents creates anxiety that could develop into real fear. My wife and I have tried to teach our children that the spirit of fear was not given to us and if there is no physical danger there is no reason to be afraid. Recently, we were watching a television program where children were hanging out and an adult stranger tried to lure them into a vehicle. Parents were behind the scenes, guessing what their kids would do in the situation and there were a lot of wrong predictions. As our kids watched we saw new dangers and what could happen. We have never told our children to fear adults, in fact we have taught our children to look an adult in the eyes and communicate with them. But you have to make them aware of the mean and evil people that are among us.

Being a coach I have seen many kids learn to cope with fear. For younger kids playing baseball, coaches are pitching so kids can hit the ball and run the bases. As I prepared them for the next step of becoming a defensive player it took a while for the concept to sink in that the pitcher on other team is trying to get them out. Kids will have a reluctance to stand in the batter's box and take pitches that are coming in from every direction.

My advice to every player is to stay in the box and if you are lucky enough to get a ball in the strike zone swing the bat. If you jump out of the box every pitch you will never have an opportunity to swing and get a hit. This is a huge obstacle for most young people but it is rewarding to see one of them get over their fear and stay in the stance and take their pitch. With young players, the pitch might be wild but it is coming in slow. Getting hit by a pitch might sting a bit but you are on your way to first base.

When the scripture was being recorded, staying in the batter's box was not God's intended message but He was telling us not to have a spirit of fear when He is on our side. Approach everything as if God was standing right next to you, protecting you and giving you sound judgment to make proper decisions. His power aligning your every thought and movement is all that you need. With the love that He projects onto and off of you there will be nothing in your way of accomplishing anything you do in His name.

In our lives, as we walk in the gospel, we all will stare down a fastball and God's instructions are clear about staying in the box. There is nothing to fear except God Himself and if we honor and follow His word the fears we stumble upon daily will be eliminated. Much of our time is spent working to provide for our families so we encounter a lot of stressful and fearful moments in the work environment. Learning to deal and handle difficult workplace decisions and issues can be overcome with the sound judgment that God grants us.

Proverbs 9:10-11 [10]The fear of the Lord, is the beginning of wisdom, and the knowledge of the Holy One is understanding. [11]For by wisdom your days will be many, and years will be added to your life.

Proverbs 9 tells us the only fear we should have is the fear of the Lord. By putting the Lord our Father first and understanding His gospel we will benefit to no end in this life. The Bible is not a very large document when you consider that within are all the words you need for instruction in life. We are not all 4.0 students or scholars, but given the power of God we can accomplish anything we desire by gathering the wisdom of the gospel He offers each and everyone of us.

Philippians 4:12-13 [12]I know both how to have a little, and I know how to have a lot. In any and all circumstances I have learned the secret of being content—whether well fed or hungry, whether in abundance or in need. [13]I am able to do all things through Him who strengthens me.

The verse Philippians 4:13 has always been one of my favorites and one of the first I ever memorized. You see it on a lot of signs and displayed by a lot of athletes. This passage can cover a multitude of situations or circumstances in your life. The message is one of strong belief and confidence from following our Lord. It can almost make you feel like a superhero when you think of the power the Lord can offer to one who believes.

Of course, this verse applies within the bounds of your own abilities. I am in my forties, so it is unlikely that if I suit up in some football gear I could convince a coach that I am ready to play ball. This plan would be outside reality but it does apply to whatever God calls you to do in your heart. If it is something you want and you are willing to go get it, the Lord will give you all the tools to get it done.

The verse just before Philippians 4:13 is often omitted and we do not get the full picture of what the Gospel is trying to convey.

Philippians 4:12 sets up the confidence and power that the Lord can bring: "I know both how to have a little, and I know how to have a lot. In any and all circumstances I have learned the secret of being content." This shows the endurance needed to succeed in any endeavor. For example, there has never been a player in football who can go out and give a two hundred yard rushing game every week. Some games are outstanding and others are average but it is the bad games that teach the player to persevere and improve.

These two verses give great insight into how to succeed in whatever you are doing. With the Lord on your team there is nothing that you cannot accomplish. Whether in sports, business or family, no one is going to deliver an all-star performance day in and day out. The ups and downs will be constant. Learn to be satisfied, whatever your circumstances, and remember at the low points that God allows you to do anything through Him that strengthens you.

I am sure everyone has been told, "Don't worry," but it is definitely easier said than done. We worry about things every day. Our lives are filled with problems related to children, money, marriage, employment, etc. that lead to worry. Whatever the concern, it is an easy path to follow to offer up your concerns to the Lord.

> **Philippians 4:6-7** ⁶Don't worry about anything, but in everything, through prayer and petition with thanksgiving, let your requests be made known to God. ⁷And the peace of God, which surpasses every thought, will guard your hearts and your minds in Christ Jesus.

The term "worry yourself to death" can become a reality if you spend every waking moment worrying about a problem.

The words "Don't worry about it" provide little comfort when you have lost your job or you do not have enough money to pay your bills. The light at the end of the tunnel does not look bright when you're staring at financial ruin. But, no matter how bad your financial situation, it does not compare to the family facing a serious health issue. When facing these circumstances it sounds ridiculous to say "Don't worry."

This is where God steps in. As His child He gives comforting instruction by telling you, "Don't worry about anything, but in everything, through prayer and petition with thanksgiving, let your requests be made known to God." God wants you to first turn to Him and present your needs to Him. With His power and works you can overcome anything, you just have to be willing to walk with and be His child.

I know life will never be worry-free but I lean on the Lord and present my problems and worries to Him first. At the bottom of my worry list are finances and money. Money is not life or death and will not buy your way into heaven. Scripture clearly states, in many verses, that God will provide for His children. This does not mean you can lie back and wait for the abundant blessings to overflow when the Lord delivers all your needs. You have to work to have food, clothing and shelter for your family.

Proverbs 19:15 Laziness induces deep sleep, and a lazy person will go hungry.

16

Conclusion

Acts 17:24-29 ²⁴The God who made the world and everything in it—He is Lord of heaven and earth and does not live in shrines made by hands. ²⁵Neither is He served by humans hands, as though He needed anything, since He Himself gives everyone life and breath and all things. ²⁶From one man he has made every nation of men to live all over the earth and has determined their appointed times and the boundaries of where they live, ²⁷so that they might seek God, and perhaps they might reach out and find Him, though He is not far from each one of us. ²⁸For in Him we live and move and exist, as even some of your own poets have said, "For we are also His offspring." ²⁹Being God's offspring, then, we shouldn't think that the divine nature is like gold or silver or stone, an image fashioned by human art and imagination.

Our family prays the same prayer before we leave the house every day. If my wife or I are out of town, or if the kids are spending the night at their grandparents' house we will still dial in to a conference call and say the prayer over the phone. It is a prayer that includes our requests and gives thanks to the Lord on a daily basis. If we do not offer our daily worship and petitions to the Lord I think we are not giving Him the honor and praise of which He is worthy. Below is the prayer we as a family say together.

> Dear Lord, thank you for this day and thank you for all your many blessings.
>
> Please forgive us of our sins and help us to forgive others.
>
> Lord please keep us be safe according to Your word which says Your angels have been given charge over us to keep us in all our ways; they will bear us up in their hands less we dash our foot against a stone.
>
> No evil shall befall us, no plague shall come near our tent.
>
> And we agree we are debt free and we have $1,380,000 to pay off all our bills.
>
> And Dear Lord please help us to be a blessing to at least one person today and please give us wisdom.
>
> In Jesus' mighty name we pray, Amen.

This is a short, basic prayer that gives us the comfort of knowing our Lord is there for us on a daily basis. If you ask for His wisdom, safety and blessings every day you can experience the guidance and protection He wants to give you.

As to the dollar amount we use in our prayer, it was derived from the debt we owed at the time. The actual number has changed over the years but we have stayed with the original figure since everyone in the family knows that number. On occasion, one of our parents have been with us in the morning and heard the prayer, so they know the number as well. The last time my mom heard us pray, she asked, "Has that number not gone down any?" We continue to pay off our debt as part of our walk with the Lord.

I have talked about many experiences in this book and hope some will help you find financial stability. Remember, finances are just one part of your overall well-being and the most important thing should be your focus on walking with God. In return, you will have the everlasting life promised by the Lord for those who follow His word.

I am just one person telling about my problems and the mistakes I have made. There are thousands of others that can offer advice and life lessons based on their own experiences, but how we relate to, and take the advice of other people does not compare to the authority and true direction that can only be received through the Gospel. Just open, read and practice what is in the Bible and you can be assured that any difficulties that come your way will be overcome by the work of the Lord.

There are many books and how-to guides on the subject of money and finances. Some can be more helpful than others on our journey to financial security and success. But, if you do not insert the Word that God as laid out you will not carry out the true plan that He has for you. His authority is supreme and will direct you to the true path that He has in His Word. There will be good times and bad times throughout your life, but no matter the situation, God is with you. You only need to accept Him and He will never deny you as your protector and savior. I would not know how to survive if I did not have the promise of His guidance and protection.

> **Ecclesiastes 7:14** In the day of prosperity be joyful, but in the day of adversity, consider: without question God has made the one as well as the other, so that man cannot discover anything that will come after him.

I wrote this book to give some insight into God's approach and practices regarding finances and money. In reality, He puts it close to the bottom in actual importance compared to the other things we should care about. Money is just hay and stubble and the rules are very simple on the approach we should take to managing the gifts and rewards we receive in our daily life. We won't survive without some form of income or cash on hand and the decisions we make will dictate how much we struggle with finances in our life on earth.

God is more concerned with our soul and making sure we live with Him throughout eternity. His love for us does not guarantee us a fancy home or a large bank account, but he does say that He will give us His word and instructions to grant us the ultimate reward of being in heaven with Him. The rules for finances are simple instructions for living. Work hard, do not borrow or have debt, give without expectation of repayment, offer assistance to those truly in need and give to the Lord what is His. In reality it is all HIS, so do not hold on tightly to the possessions of which you are only a steward.

Hopefully, my words and experiences will help you get better control of your financial and spiritual life. I have included a lot of scriptures to give you some insight into God's word. I hope this will not only aid your understanding of what the Gospel says but also draw you closer to the Lord who truly loves you and wants nothing but good things for you in your life.

If this book draws one person to turn their life over to God it has been a worthwhile task. In the end, it is not about our finances but the way God wants us to live and follow His Word that He offers us truly free of charge. If we follow a few simple daily practices we can show Him our everlasting appreciation for what He has done for us. His love for us is beyond what we can imagine.

www.ingramcontent.com/pod-product-compliance
Lightning Source LLC
Chambersburg PA
CBHW020654300426
44112CB00007B/380